Two Ruddy Ducks

and a

Partridge on a Par Three

The Unexpurgated Golf Letters of Mortimer Merriweather

Clive Agran

MERLIN UNWIN BOOKS

First published in Great Britain by Merlin Unwin Books Ltd 2023

Merlin Unwin Books Ltd
Palmers House
7 Corve Street
Ludlow
Shropshire SY8 1DB
UK

www.merlinunwin.co.uk

ISBN 978 1 913159 70 2
Design, edited and typset in 11.5 point Adobe Caslon Pro by
Joanne Dovey, Merlin Unwin Books
Printed by TJ Books, Padstow

Special thanks to another struggling hacker, Tony Husband.
Perhaps most famous for creating the Yobs in *Private Eye*,
the 18-handicapper has added his own humorous
perspective by contributing some cracking cartoons.

Foreword

Mortimer is busy ironing his plus fours at the moment and has therefore asked me to pen this foreword. As you can tell from the number of pages that you will shortly have to plough through, the old boy has fired off a fair few letters of late and his gnarled and aged fingers will therefore benefit from a break.

Before I go any further, there are a few things I should perhaps explain to you about Mortimer. Reading his letters, you might form the impression that here is a grumpy old geezer with too much time on his hands and nothing better to do than vent his frustration at his increasing inability to reach a fairway or escape from a bunker by annoying those in authority with his daft ideas and ridiculous suggestions. Well, you would absolutely right because that succinctly sums him up.

As his age and handicap inexorably rise, Mortimer is undoubtedly becoming somewhat disenchanted with the world. However, although some of his letters display what appears to be intolerance, please don't be offended. A combination of gout and the yips has undoubtedly warped his mind but the upside of that is he has developed an entirely original perspective that has endowed him with a unique outlook. He's very much a man of his time unequipped to cope with political correctness, woke awareness or anything originating much after 1957.

In any case I don't want to sound too negative as, when you eventually get around to reading his letters, you may well be impressed with his originality and forthrightness. He thinks of things that would almost certainly never occur to any right-minded person.

Now might be a good time to explain why there aren't any replies to be found in the following pages. Well, with one or two honourable exceptions, they were just too dull.

Mortimer concentrates on golf because that has been the main focus of his life ever since his great grandfather Egbert left him a mashie-niblick in his will. Golf, together with Madeira wine and the occasional port, is what he lives for. Not content with having won two monthly medals and one mid-week seniors' Stableford in his four-score years, he has sought to bolster his legacy with the letters contained in this book.

Whether the name Merriweather rightfully belongs alongside Old Tom Morris, Ben Hogan, Jack Nicklaus and Tiger Woods in the pantheon of golfing greats is for you to decide. It might sound a preposterous notion now but wait until you've read this book before you make up your mind about the merits of Mortimer Merriweather.

Clive Agran

Curated Letters

To Rose, who hates golf but loves me, I think.

Dear British Trust for Ornithology

I desperately need your help in persuading the golf authorities around the world to adopt new nomenclature for describing how many shots have been taken over par. In case you're not familiar with the Royal and Ancient game, I should explain that par is what a good player on a good day should score on any particular hole. For a short hole it's three, for a medium length hole it's four and for a very long hole it's five.

Exceptionally good players can, of course, score lower than par. One below par is a birdie, two below par is an eagle and three below par is an albatross. Because you know pretty well everything there is to know about birds, you will note the avian nature of the terminology.

Good, bad and average players frequently take a lot more shots than they should on a hole – one, two, three, four, five or more. Bogey is not a particularly nice word but it's the one used to describe a score of one over par. Thereafter, the game betrays a paucity of originality by describing two over par as a double bogey, three over par as a triple bogey, etc., etc.

There is surely scope for a more imaginative nomenclature here and continuing with the avian theme is clearly both desirable and easily achieved. Having given it a great deal of thought, I have come to the conclusion that one over par, which is presently a bogey, should instead be called a 'partridge'. I like it for two principal reasons: 1) It's just a bit more than par. In fact, it's a 'tridge' more than par. And 2) It will enable players who score a four on a short hole to say, 'I had a partridge on the par three', which I think will cause much merriment.

What should also provide a lot of laughs is 'Great Tit', which I think is an apt name for what is currently called a double bogey. Thereafter, I'm hoping for suggestions from you. In case you can't think of any, I've drawn up a provisional list of what I think would work well:

Three over par – presently triple bogey – a 'Shag'.

Four over par – presently quadruple bogey – a 'Ruddy Duck'.

Five over par – presently quintuple bogey – a 'Fluffy-backed Tit Babbler'.

Although with golfers anything is possible and former British Open champion David Duval recorded a nine-over par 14 on a par five in The Open at Royal Portrush in 2019, I think we should probably stop at the 'Fluffy-backed Tit Babbler', don't you? At least golfers will be able to say things like, 'I had a couple of Great Tits on the front and finished with a Shag up the last.'

10

Dear Prince Harry,

You and I have so much in common. We both have ginger hair for starters and both have fallen out big time with our respective elder brothers. Like you, I was said to have married beneath me when I hooked up with Mavis, a hairdresser's assistant, on holiday in Bognor in 1952, the year your lovely grandmother ascended to the throne. My marriage only lasted 18 months and so, reluctant though I am to admit it, my family might have had a point after all. What's more, we're both connected with Sussex, me by residence and you by title.

And we're both published authors. Your book costs a great deal more than mine but there are a lot of photos in yours and you had to pay the geezer who wrote it and doubtless took care of the punctuation for you. But £28 is almost as much as the green fee at Dale Hill and rather a lot for just a book, don't you think? Copies are bound to start turning up in charity shops and car-boot sales before very long for a fraction of the price and so, if you don't mind, I'll pick one up later.

Until I've read it, I obviously don't know why you and William fell out. I haven't spoken to my brother since he borrowed my sand wedge in 1962 and left it in a bunker at Carnoustie. He couldn't even remember whether it was on the front or back nine let alone which precisely of the 112 bunkers it was!

Anyway, my purpose it writing to you now is to enquire whether you would be interested in cooperating with me in writing a golf instruction book. Frankly, since I would be responsible for devising all the tips as well doing all the writing, you would have even less to do than you did with *Spare*. All it will involve is posing for a few photos with a golf club in your hand. Why, you might wonder, do I need you at all? To be honest, I don't:

but you are a Royal, albeit only just, and when it comes to book sales you now have a proven track record.

For most of us ordinary people, getting a book published is harder than it was securing an invite to one of your late Grandma and Grandpa's legendary garden parties at Buckingham Palace. But if I go to a publisher and explain that the fifth in line to the throne is involved, they are going to prick up their well-educated ears and are likely to come up with an advance that'll buy Meghan – who I imagine is pretty high maintenance – quite a few frocks.

Please consider my proposal urgently. You're a relatively hot property at the moment – but for how much longer? If Meghan kicks you out or Dad cuts you off, you'll soon fade from the public's consciousness and *Harry's Hot Golf Tips* would be even less in demand than your poor old Uncle Andy.

Dear Mayor of Tunbridge Wells,

Have you ever been to Edinburgh? I wouldn't bother going. It's invariably cold and wet with, frankly, very little to see or do. I think they're horribly disfiguring but I gather the city is famous for its tattoos. It probably began with the Celts painting woad onto their bodies. Then along comes Rob Roy thinking an eagle across his shoulder blades will make him look scary and a whole industry is born to rival whisky distilling.

Fast forward several hundred years and JK Rowling bursts onto the scene with her hugely successful books, films and merchandise to give the city a whole new lease of life as Harry Potter's birthplace. Today there are countless Harry Potter trails, landmarks, gift-shops and the like that attract tens of thousands of Potterheads. Well, what JK Rowling did for Edinburgh I can do for Tunbridge Wells.

It's all a bit hush-hush at the moment but I'm extremely confident that my main character is going to be every bit as big as Harry Potter. Swap quidditch for golf and Hogwarts for Dale Hill Hotel and Country Club and you've a taste of what I'm about.

The first challenge is to write the thing. You may be aware that JK Rowling mostly knocked out her stories in cafes. Principally because they are inhabited by nattering women, I'm not especially fond of cafes and work much better in pubs. When you consider that those Edinburgh cafes that JK Rowling frequented are now attracting millions of tourists, you can surely see the phenomenal potential extra business I could generate for the Dog and Duck, Coach and Horses, etc.

Being ruthlessly commercial for a moment, what I'm essentially looking for is a contra-deal with the aforementioned hostelries whereby they supply me with complimentary beer today in exchange for becoming tourist hot-spots tomorrow. A letter from you confirming my legitimacy would, I'm sure, help convince the relevant pub landlords of the immense value of the proposed partnership.

Assuming everything goes well, there's every chance we will meet one another when they confer the Freedom of Tunbridge Wells on me for services to local tourism.

Dear Sir Nick Faldo,

Although you have won six more major championships than I have and have had two more divorces – three to my one – I think we have a lot in common. For a start we are both very keen on golf and both play right-handed. You are an only child and so am I, which is possibly quite significant because we were undoubtedly over-indulged by doting parents and you appear to be unbearably self-obsessed as a consequence.

Used to getting what we want, you strove to become the world's best golfer whereas my goal is to be captain of Dale Hill.

Burning ambition and single-minded determination are not particularly attractive qualities, especially if other people are ignored or trampled on in the quest for success. Like me, I would guess you never had many friends. Who needs them? They would only have distracted you from your obsessive focus on winning. Another plus was your apparent unconcern about being enormously unpopular with your fellow competitors

It was your second wife Gill who revealed that the births of her three children by you were all induced to avoid any clashes with your playing schedule. Every bloke whose golf is severely curtailed because of 'partner considerations' will doff his peaked cap in admiration. Possibly still a little resentful, Gill once said of you, 'Socially, he was a 24-handicapper.' Hell hath no fury, eh Nick? Oops, forgive me, Sir Nick.

You were an exceptionally successful golfer, does it matter you're a cold fish that made extraordinarily embarrassing speeches and were arguably the most incompetent Ryder Cup captain of all time? Not to you, I suspect, because you have three claret jugs on your mantelpiece and three green jackets in your wardrobe that would appear to vindicate your whole approach to life in general and golf in particular.

Anyway, I'm starting a golf society exclusively for those of us who are unloved, socially inept, lack empathy and ordinarily struggle to find anyone to play with. It's called the Friendless And Letsbehonest Decidedly Odd (FALDO) golf society and I'm hoping you will consider becoming our honorary president.

Dear R&A Rules Adjudicating Committee,

There was a complicated incident in the second round of the Spring Mixed Foursomes Blenkinsopp Shield at Dale Hill Hotel and Golf Club that has baffled our in-house rules' expert and so, in desperation, I turn to you for a definitive ruling.

I was partnering Frieda Witherspoon against Reginald and Cynthia Spleen. We were three up after only four holes when Cynthia sliced her tee shot at the fifth into a thicket just to the right of a lateral water hazard. Realising that it might be lost, Reg teed up another ball, declared it a provisional but, already somewhat annoyed, missed the ball completely. Cynthia then stepped up and stated that the tee-peg was too high for her, declared the ball unplayable, took a penalty drop within two clubs' length and topped the proceeding shot into a flooded bunker. Reg angrily declared the ball unplayable and kicked it out of the hazard into an area designated as 'Ground Under Repair.' Furious with her partner, Cynthia claimed relief but mistakenly dropped the ball more than one club length away from the edge of the 'GUR' white line. Before the next shot was taken, Reg drew this infringement to our attention at which point Cynthia struck him on the head with a seven iron thereby inadvertently changing the club's characteristics and causing a gaping wound to open in Reg's forehead that, coincidentally, subsequently required seven stitches.

Should my partner and I have: a) claimed the hole before anyone else got hurt; b) disappeared into the thicket under the pretext of looking for the original ball and let the other pair just get on with it; or c) claimed the match under the Rules of Equity and walked in? Well, we did c) but omitted to mark our ball before retiring to the bar and the Spleens, on realising this, similarly claimed the match.

Which pair should proceed into the third round to face the formidable Fescue-Greens?

Dear North Face,

I've been looking in your catalogue for the very largest tent you manufacture. Am I right in thinking it's the Summit Series Two Metre Dome? At £6,200 it's hardly cheap. I could buy a second-hand Vauxhall Corsa for that money but, there again, it would be something of a struggle to sleep eight people inside it. Back to your tent which, frankly, is nowhere near big enough for the purpose I have in mind.

Let me explain. As anyone who has ever lived in this country for any length of time will know, potholes apart, the real problem with Britain is the weather. Maybe in 25 years' time when global warming has really kicked in, things will be better but right now our weather is simply not good enough and has a serious negative impact on outdoor sporting events.

They've sorted it at Wimbledon by installing a roof over the Centre and Number One courts. And what a boon they've proved. The biggest beneficiary is TV. Watching puddles accumulate on the covers or, worse still, listening to Cliff Richard singing, is thankfully a thing of the past. Nowadays when you switch on the television to watch good old Andy Murray's mouth wide open as he yells at his box, that's what you get.

Although it presents unique problems, I think the next sport that would benefit most from excluding the elements when they turn hostile is golf. Not only is rain very unpleasant, it's also a serious problem, not least because it makes the grips wet and the clubs hard to hold. Umbrellas help but they're not the complete answer. And then there's the wind that can make it difficult to judge which club to take. It can also blow a ball away from where you wanted it to go, which is really annoying.

The solution is an enormous tent that can be quickly erected when the weather turns nasty. Your Summit Series Two Metre Dome tent only covers a little over 15 square metres whereas, for example, the Old Course at St Andrews will require roughly 1,618,740 square metres. Presumably, there will be significant economies of scale otherwise I calculate the Summit Series 1,618,740 Metre Dome would cost an eye-watering £10 billion. Any clubs on The Open rota interested would be well advised to wait until one of Blacks' summer sales when 25% off would save them a whopping £2.5 billion.

Dear Mr Disney,

Below is the synopsis of a feel-good movie I think you should make. It has the working title 'Caught Cheating'. I don't want millions for it, just a modest $100,000 and a decent part in the film.

The action takes place in Surrey, England in 2019.

To the outsider, Charles Salisbury's life seems perfect. Married to the lovely and very much younger Linda, he has two delightful children, a secure job with a bank and is considered a pillar of the local community. His crowning moment comes at a dinner at his golf club held to celebrate his appointment as captain. However, his world starts to fall apart when, minutes before he is due to make his acceptance speech, he is caught literally with his pants down in the locker room with Geoffrey, the new assistant greenkeeper.

He's thrown out of the marital home by his humiliated wife, sacked by the bank, expelled from his club and, worse still, he finds his favourite Ping putter (product placement opportunity) broken and stuffed in a dustbin. Although almost broken himself, this last act of wanton vandalism motivates him to fight back.

With what little money he has, he buys a caravan and camps on a strip of a wasteland adjoining the local municipal golf course. Unlike the toffs at his old club, the less stuffy working-class members of the municipal club welcome him. Driven by a burning desire to revenge his humiliation and with little else to do, he practises golf for hours every day and improves bit by bit. He captains the team at his new club in their annual match against his old club and, fired by all that has happened, his inspirational leadership helps his team to their first-ever success in the fixture.

Charles, however, doesn't stop there. Despite being over 40, his handicap tumbles to scratch but, because of what happened that night, he's never picked to play for his county. Then, against the odds, he comes through both a pre-qualifier and qualifier to earn a spot in the British Open. Despite a double-bogey six at the first hole, he has rounds of 69 and 67 to comfortably make the cut. After each round he returns to his caravan, which he tows behind his beaten-up old car. Alone, he stares at photos of his ex-wife, son and daughter, and sobs.

Another 67 in the third round puts him in contention and he tees off on the last day in the final pairing, still symbolically eschewing a caddy and pulling a trolley. As he sinks a 20-foot putt on the last hole to clinch The Open, he sees his wife, son and daughter cheering in the stands as he lifts the claret jug as the end credits roll.

I think Brad Pitt would make an excellent Charles Salisbury and Keira Knightley would be ideal as his wife. I'm not fussed about which part I'm given so long as I get to play a bit of golf.

Dear President Putin,

At the time of writing, your decision to launch a 'special military operation' against Ukraine is not looking terribly clever. But we all make mistakes. In a desperate attempt to reach the green of the par five 11th hole at Dale Hill in three,

I once famously tried to hit a driver off the deck in the second round of the Veterans Mid-Week Autumn Shield, chunked the ball into the ditch and eventually had to settle for an eight. So, although I've never been directly responsible for the death of tens of thousands of innocent people, I can imagine how you feel. And I have served on the Greens Committee of the aforementioned Dale Hill when Reginald Blenkinsopp was captain and so have some idea of how despotic regimes operate.

Fortunately, Blenkinsopp's tyrannical reign only lasted 12 months whereas you've been running the show in Russia for more than a quarter of a century and so no-one could complain if you said you had had enough of poisoning your opponents, orchestrating corruption, abusing human rights and causing unimaginable pain and suffering.

However, you don't strike me as the sort who would happily retire to a cosy dacha in the country to live quietly off the billions of roubles you've doubtless salted away. If nothing else, it would be a waste of the sporting super-hero image you've so carefully cultivated over your lifetime. But ice hockey, judo and all the other macho activities you have focused on are not really suitable for a septuagenarian, even one as evidently psychotic as you are.

Might I suggest that the time has come to cash in on the fortuitous fact that your surname sounds like 'putt-in'. In case you're unfamiliar with the bourgeois sport of golf, putting is the single most important part of the game; it's often described as the game within a game. Briefly, it's the crucial bit where you have to knock the ball into the hole. Even though they don't know much about golf and are only interested in having a laugh, a lot of people enjoy putting on what we call 'crazy golf courses'. Although, thank God, very few people are as crazy as you, there is almost certainly a huge money-making opportunity for you to exploit.

Why don't you convert the numerous plush properties you're rumoured to own into a chain of 'President Putin's Putting Palaces'? Each could have its own separate theme. You could have a 'Nasty NATO' course where, for example, on the opening hole you have to knock the ball into an American Abrams tank so that it runs along the barrel of the gun before plopping out harmlessly at the end. Together with a rusting nuclear missile that clearly will never leave the ground, these holes would dramatically expose NATO's bluff.

Another course could be dedicated to 'Great Russian Despots' which would feature life-size models of such heroes as Lenin, Stalin, Ivan the Terrible and, of course, yourself on the prestigious finishing hole. Another necessarily short course could showcase Russia's allies. The possibilities are almost as endless as the prison sentences meted out to your hapless opponents.

This imaginative proposal might just rehabilitate your reputation sufficiently so that you will principally be remembered as the man who introduced crazy golf to Russia rather than the brutal megalomaniac who deserves to rot in hell.

Dear Sunningdale,

A very good friend of mine, who presently lives in Dubai, has decided that, in future, he will divide his time between the UAE in winter and England in summer. He has chosen England as his second home because he is passionate about golf and believes we have the finest courses in the world.

A man of considerable substance, he is president of a substantial energy company, extraordinarily wealthy, lives in an enormous house with 15 bedrooms, owns half-a-dozen Rolls Royces and at least two yachts.

An absolute pillar of middle-eastern society, he is on first-name terms with the ruling royal family in the UAE, gives vast sums of money to charity and is the honorary president of one that provides golf equipment and lessons to disadvantaged Emirati kids.

Apart from finding him a mansion in Surrey and a large flat in Knightsbridge, I have been given the awesome responsibility of selecting a suitable golf club that not only has a world-class course but is also enormously prestigious. Sunningdale seems ideal.

As he's a past captain of Dubai Creek Golf and Yacht Club, a member of the R&A and a scratch golfer, I assume that being accepted by Sunningdale would be a pure formality. The only slight issue might be what type of membership he should apply for and I would therefore be most grateful if you would confirm that family membership would include his six wives, 15 children and 22 grandchildren.

Dear Chubby Chandler,

Forgive me if I come across as rather excited, but I have just won my club's monthly midweek Stableford. It's the second Stableford that I've won in 12 months and has served to underline the dramatic improvement I have made since wrapping my right hand much further over my left thumb.

It's a tip Guy Lambert, a regular member of our Sunday morning group, gave me and I dedicated my recent win to him in gratitude.

Anyway, I'm writing to you to find out if you're interested in becoming my agent. You see there are already, and I hope you don't mind me saying this, too many top-class players who play extremely well. What the game needs, in my opinion, is someone of lesser ability like myself. Why do I say that? Because it is far easier for the average club golfer out there to identify with someone like me, rather than a tour pro who hits the ball out of sight.

You see, I play in a way the public understands and can relate to. What I'm saying is that I believe golf needs someone refreshingly different from the all-too-consistent-and-ridiculously-steady professionals who presently dominate the game. And that someone could be me.

With a handicap of 19 and without your help it wouldn't, of course, be easy for me to get to play in the big events, let alone make cuts and secure top 10 finishes. However, as something of a curiosity, I might obtain a few sponsors' invites and wildcard entries in the same way that Annika Sorenstam and that 14-year-old Hawaiian girl did all those years ago. If all else fails, I could always have a crack at the Asian tour.

Dear TaylorMade,

Once a gifted 17 handicapper who was solid both off the tee and around the greens, I'm now struggling to break 100. Why? To put it bluntly, my body is letting me down. More specifically, it's my left hip. Arthritis has taken its toll and the nice people at my local hospital are now telling me that I need to replace it, presumably with a shiny new one, which is where you come in.

Instead of any old 'off-the-shelf' hip, I'd like a customised one specifically designed to, yes, improve my golf! Why, I thought to myself as I sat in the hospital waiting-room, can't my hip match my clubs? If I can play with forged-iron, cavity-back clubs, why can't I walk on a similarly designed hip with the same level of performance and forgiving properties? If, for example, my hip had the same coefficient of restitution as my driver, is it not reasonable to assume that I could sit down, get up and walk around with the same assuredness with which I drive off the tee?

And a graphite shaft connecting my hip to my femur should ensure I recover the sort of flexibility my body enjoyed 30 years

ago. And what a psychological boost it would be to know that my hip and clubs were not only totally compatible but were manufactured by the very same people.

I appreciate that producing body parts is not an area into which you have ventured but, given the worrying decline in the number of people playing golf, wouldn't it be sensible to diversify? I'm sure all those white-coated boffins you presently employ to expand the sweet-spot could easily turn their educated hands to reducing human suffering whilst at the same time rescuing veteran golfers from the indignity of a 20+ handicap.

If it encourages you to take up my suggestion, I would happily let you fit me with the very first TaylorMade hip in the world and have my game monitored to see what, if any, improvements followed.

Although I'm not sure whether or not you could sell them in pro shops, I am absolutely certain that artificial hips are a booming market that will surely continue to expand as the population ages.

Dear US Masters Organising Committee,

Before I reveal my exciting idea, I should like to say what a great tournament you put on. It's a highlight of my year and it's just a shame that it comes in April as, apart from The Open in July, there's nothing much else to look forward to this side of Christmas.

My one criticism of the US Masters is that it's all a bit 'samey'. You might want to consider moving it around to different courses as I suspect TV viewers are growing a bit bored with Amen Corner, azaleas and pine straw. I've an idea: instead of it always being green, how about rotating a range of colours for the winner's jacket? Or, better still, let the winner choose. It would be fun trying to guess whether he would go for the Day-Glo orange, imperial purple or a rainbow-coloured one to show support for the LBGTQIA movement. And think how much more interesting it would be from a visual point of view if the past winners wore different, brightly-coloured jackets instead of the same dreary green.

Anyway, my principal point is that I can't help thinking that you're missing a huge and valuable trick by not capitalising on what are known as naming rights. You see it everywhere in sport these days, with stadiums and tournaments bearing the name of what is called in the business, a title sponsor. You would be astonished at the sort of sums companies are prepared to cough up just to have their name linked to a big sporting occasion. And, without wishing to flatter you, yours is most definitely a very big sporting occasion.

Obviously you would need to think very carefully about what sort of title sponsor you want. Because your tournament is watched right around the world, you ought to be searching for what is known as a global brand.

So who would be suitable? Well, when I think of America I think of unbelievably stupid gun laws that allow nutters to needlessly mow down dozens of innocent people every year. Leaving that to one side, what else is there that is quintessentially American? Well, hamburgers of course. And when you think of hamburgers, two big names spring to mind. I've ruled out McDonald's because they will almost certainly want to erect a giant golden arch above Magnolia Drive and I appreciate that a few of your less enlightened members might not be too happy with that. And so how about the almost equally well-known Burger King? It's as American as Donald Trump and has plenty of bucks to spend on marketing. One massive inducement you could offer is to change the title you bestow upon whoever wins from the US Masters Champion to the Burger Meister, geddit?

○○○○○

Dear Jon Rahm,

I must confess to envying professional golfers. When I'm trudging through the mud on a nippy old day with the wind whistling around my hearing aids and the icy rain penetrating my so-called waterproofs, you lot are invariably somewhere ridiculously warm and sunny. The only downside to playing golf when it's hot is one can get rather sweaty, which can be extremely unpleasant for your caddie and playing partners.

The answer I've come up with is a dedicated range of specialised fragrances designed specifically with smelly golfers in mind. Because it sounds a bit like 'Ram', Rahm has just the right sexual overtone that is the fashion with fragrances these days. Long gone is the era of Old Spice, now it's all Amour, Passion, Submissive and Climax. What do you think of 'Rahm Pour Homme – the Sweet Smell of Success'?

I'm getting a bit ahead of myself because I haven't even mentioned that I am developing a unique range of fragrances suitable for all golfers, irrespective of handicap. There are four principal scents each named after a category of course: 'dune', 'parkland', 'woodland' and 'municipal'. Grass is the principal odour in all of them but there's a definite whiff of the sea in 'dune', flowers in 'parkland', pine in 'woodland' and diesel fumes in 'municipal' They are on a sliding price scale with 'dune' the most expensive and 'municipal' comfortably in the budget bracket.

In order for the tag line – *The Sweet Smell of Success* – to be appropriate, I obviously need the support and endorsement of a successful golfer. As you're world number one at the time of writing, I thought it only fair to approach you first. So long as you are in the top ten, there'll be no problem but the draft contract that I will happily post to your agent does contain an escape clause that I may activate when, as is unfortunately inevitable one day, you slip to 11th or lower. Although that sounds harsh, in practice I will allow a four-week period of grace in which, should you scramble back inside the top ten, the contract, which incidentally obliges you to dab on 'Rahm Pour Homme' before and after every round, to continue. And it might be helpful if you could carry a few bottles with you at all times, as cash sales provide a welcome income boost.

Dear Justin Thomas,

May I first of all, congratulate you on your excellent golf.

From tee to green you are undoubtedly one of the top players around at the moment. And, if you continue to practise conscientiously, I see no reason why you shouldn't improve and put yourself out there alongside some of the all-time greats like Jack Nicholson.

However, watching you on Sky television playing in a recent tournament in the US, I couldn't help but notice that you were tending to bend your right arm as you near the top of your backswing. In this respect, you've got the same problem as my mate Reg, who plays off 21.

Both you and he tend to spray the ball a bit when you do this. Frankly he does it more than you do but, there again, you take the game a lot more seriously than he does.

It helps Reg to imagine he's got a broom handle stuffed down the right sleeve of his shirt. You might care to try this and see if it makes a difference.

Lastly, I understand that you're finally about to get married to Jillian Wisniewski. Congratulations. However, don't make the mistake I did and not tell your intended about your fondness for golf. I suggest you sit down quietly one evening, explain that you play a lot of golf and that this means you will be away quite a bit. In this way, you'll prepare her a bit better than I did my wife and avoid the ridiculous arguments every time you go off to play.

Dear Scottish Tourist Board,

I'm thinking of going to Scotland next year for a holiday. I've never been before and, although I gather it can be very cold, even in summer, I would like to give it a try, if for no other reason than to find out what the kilted people really think of Humza Yousaf. I believe he would have won the SNP leadership contest more comfortably if he'd changed his name to Humza McYousaf.

With all the turmoil facing the Scot Nats, he'll probably soon be off to live somewhere warm, sunny and tax-free like that other Scottish patriot, Sean Connery – who is now back in Scotland after having his ashes scattered over the famous links of St Andrews. I wonder if they realise that, under rule 23, if a bit of him lands on a green, it may be regarded as a loose impediment and removed without penalty, which is a bit of an ignominious end for a former James Bond.

Back to business. I took up golf about 50 years ago and, due to a combination of natural talent and sheer determination, have steadily reduced my handicap to the 19.4 it is today. Anyway, I'm considering taking my half-set of clubs with me to Scotland but don't want to use up precious space in my little Fiat if there aren't any decent courses up there. Do you know if there are? I appreciate it's unfair to compare countries but I went to Croatia last year and found a couple of real beauties right next to the Adriatic. Are there any in Scotland next to the sea?

A couple of other things. Do you know if the rules are the same in Scotland as they are in England? I would hate to embarrass myself by accusing some poor jock of cheating if he's only doing something that's allowed north of the border. For example, I expect you're given more time to look for a lost ball up there. Finally, I understand Scotland has its own currency and bank notes. Would I do better changing my money in England or is the exchange rate no different in Scotland?

Dear Bernhard Langer,

In my opinion, the enormous success you have achieved in golf over half a century has demonstrated that, despite losing back-to-back world wars, Germany is still capable of producing winners. Only Boris Becker comes close to matching your sporting achievements but his recent spell inside disqualifies him from even being considered as Germany's greatest modern athlete. It's perhaps testament to my admiration for you that I can even find it within me to forgive you missing that straightforward six-footer that cost Europe the Ryder Cup at Kiawah Island in 1989. I had £10 on Europe to win at 15/8 but, don't worry, I'm very nearly over it now.

Your direct, almost mechanical, no-nonsense approach to the game was in stark contrast to Seve's incredible flair and flamboyance. It was Teutonic efficiency versus Latin exuberance. Your autobiography, unimaginatively entitled *My Autobiography*, exemplifies this straightforward, unfussy attitude. In it you explain how you overcame the dreaded putting yips no fewer than four times in your career, which is both astonishing and why I'm writing to you now.

Sadly, not everybody is endowed with the same mental fortitude with which you are evidently blessed and therefore aren't able to overcome the awful affliction in the way you did. These unfortunates need help. I'm delighted to say that I can offer it in the shape of the greatest golf training aid ever invented, the Yipstick.

Looking exactly like a regular putter, the Yipstick has a powerful lithium battery in the grip and a randomiser in the putting blade connected to it. Scientific research has revealed that it's having to take back the putter head that creates the tension in both the biceps and triceps of the sufferer, which leads to an involuntary muscle spasm that causes the yip. By transmitting a powerful electric charge at an indeterminate moment anywhere between five and 25 seconds after the putter head has touched the ground at address, the Yipstick sends a potent electric signal to the muscles to contract and thus effectively takes over control of the putting stroke.

There's no point in pretending that using a Yipstick is anything other than extremely unpleasant but that in itself is its greatest virtue. Players regularly receiving between 125 and 175 volts in both arms, rapidly reach the conclusion that they would rather risk a yip than continue with the Yipstick. After ditching it and no longer having to worry about receiving any further electric shocks, players relax so thoroughly that, somewhat miraculously, the anxiety evaporates and they no longer yip their putts.

The Yipstick will retail for €199 (not including battery). For a generous 2% of nett revenue, would you consider endorsing it?

Dear Lloyd's of London,

I presume most, if not all, of your members are golfers. Even the women! That's a good thing because golfers more than any other category of human being understand the tricky business of risk/reward. For example, there's a pond guarding the green on a par four and to carry the pond and reach the green is a distance of, say, 148 yards. Do you take out a wood and go for it or lay up with something safe like a five iron? That's the sort of tricky risk/reward calculation we golfers have to make somewhere in the region of 18 times a round.

And golfers understand the nature of insurance better than, say, tennis players because, 1) an errant golf shot can do a lot more damage than a mistimed volley, and 2) tennis players can't score a hole-in-one and are therefore never required to buy a round of drinks for a large bunch of thirsty strangers.

The other factor that I know will enhance the appeal of the proposal I'm about to make is that golf club membership is ridiculously expensive and, if you join an absurdly posh club with top-notch facilities such as fresh towels in the changing room, it can run into thousands of pounds. But what happens if, as we have discovered to our considerable cost recently, there's a global pandemic? You can't play golf and nor can you claim a refund. An extended lockdown, in effect, costs you a considerable sum of money but not if you have taken out a pandemic policy.

Someone who has shelled out, say, £2000 on his annual golf club membership surely won't baulk at paying a modest £100 on top to insure himself against not being able to play because of some nasty virus. It will be hugely profitable not only because these things only occur on average about once a century but also because, as we all know, you boys are hugely adept at finding reasons for not paying out. You could, for example shove a clause in the small print that says, inter alia, that you're only liable if the lockdown lasts for more than three months, which is most unlikely, and the first two months aren't covered anyway. Kerching!

All I ask is for a modest 10% commission on all the premiums. Interested?

Dear Professional Golfers Association of America,

I appreciate that in some energetic sports a build-up of phlegm in the mouth can occur that, where the individual concerned is reluctant to swallow aforementioned unpleasant substance, he or she may feel it necessary to spit. However, even when played quite quickly, which is, sadly, never the case in your events, golf isn't one of those sports and it is therefore completely unnecessary for the participants to do it. And so why do they, especially when millions of people all over the world are watching? What sort of example is that setting children? During the final round of the USPGA this year, I counted no fewer than seven, full-blown gobs, as we call them in the UK. Keegan Bradley, Kevin Kisner, Tiger Woods, Justin Johnson... the bigger the name, the more it seems they feel the need to spit.

Although I don't want to make too big a thing of it, it's dramatically less prevalent among European golfers. For example, I've never seen Justin Rose, Rory McIlroy or even the slightly wild Tommy Fleetwood indulge in this disgusting practice so there is evidently a cultural element involved here.

Having thought long and hard about the subject, I have rejected the idea of installing spittoons next to every tee and green as this would add unsightly clutter. Instead, I have come to the conclusion there is no alternative but to penalise players: one shot if the offence takes place on the tee, fairway or in the rough; two on the green and three if anyone is audacious enough to gob into the hole. That would pretty soon put a stop to it!

As I suspect you will be too pusillanimous for such decisive action, I have an alternative proposal. The scorers who accompany each group in the majors should be tasked with the responsibility of noting down every time a player spits. Then, at the end of the tournament, the 'winner' could be presented with the 'Silver Spitoon'; in other words, publicly humiliated.

Dear St George's Hill,

Those of us who love sport appreciate what a marvellously civilizing influence it can be. There are so many lessons that sport can teach us: self-discipline, magnanimity, confidence, graciousness, getting along with team-mates and accepting decisions. And there really is nothing like the delicious pleasure of crushing opponents, is there?

'Sport in the Community' deals with what are commonly termed 'problem children'. Almost exclusively from deprived backgrounds, they are simply kids who, through no fault of their own, find themselves at odds with society. Mostly they are just petty criminals who thieve and deal in drugs because they've never been shown a better way. Frequently disowned by their families and shunned by society, there's a real danger they will be consigned to life's waste-bin unless something dramatic is done to encourage them to mend their ways and change their lives.

Those of us involved in 'Sport in the Community' passionately believe we can rescue these children through sport. With responsibility for most of south-east London, I have so far managed to persuade various providers of sporting facilities to contribute at least some time to our youngsters. They include a ten-pin bowling alley, roller-skating rink, gym and swimming pool. Having identified golf as a suitable activity, I'm very much hoping you will be willing to help as well.

All we ask is that our boys and girls are welcomed at your club on, say, one or two days a week – preferably including a Saturday and/or Sunday – and are made to feel at home. Although to the best of my knowledge none has played golf before, most are willing to experiment and give it a go. If you could lend them the sticks and balls, I'm sure they would be happy to take it from there. We wouldn't presume to ask that you supervise them but it might be as well to keep a general eye on proceedings.

It would, of course, be wonderful if we discovered the next Mick Faldo but I'm much more concerned that our kids learn that success has to be earned; a lesson I hope they will learn observing and mixing with your high achieving members.

Dear Prostatitis Sufferers' Association,

Normally large is a good thing. For example, a large portion of chips is better than a small portion, unless you're trying to lose weight, of course. But an enlarged prostate is, as we all know, really bad news as, apart from any other considerations, it means you have to wee far more often than non-sufferers.

Life can become awkward and embarrassing. One tip you might care to pass on to your members is to only wear dark trousers; the darker the better. But it's with regard to sport in general and golf in particular that I'm writing to you now.

Not unnaturally, men with prostatitis want to live as normal a life as possible and that includes participating in sport. But not all sports are prostatically friendly, so to speak. Take athletics, for example. Some events are clearly not as inclusive as they should be and, in effect, discriminate against those with enlarged prostates. The 10,000 metres can take well over half an hour, particularly if you're a bit slow. And that might be just too long for some. So why not persuade the athletic authorities to pause the race half-way so that those that need to, can go to the toilet?

Tennis has been leading the way in this regard by allowing players to more or less go to the loo whenever they want. Sadly this progressive policy has led to a fair bit of abuse where players claim to need the toilet but are just leaving the court to break their opponent's concentration. I would suggest to the LTA and ATP that they should furnish each player with a sample jar that has to be filled by those requesting a break. Failure to fill it should cost offenders at least a set.

The only sport that really caters for prostatitis sufferers is golf. Even though a round can take upwards of four hours, there are innumerable opportunities for players to relieve themselves in the trees and bushes. Links courses, which are in any case hugely over-rated and frequently prohibitively expensive, offer little cover in this regard and are therefore best avoided.

In conclusion, therefore, I would urge you to adopt golf as the official sport of the Prostatitis Sufferers' Association

Dear Penguin Books,

Love him or hate him, undoubtedly one of the most influential characters of the last century was Adolf Hitler. There have, I know, been an awful lot of books about him but none so far has explored what I think was a critical influence on him … golf. My book, *Golf and the Rise of Fascism*, examines the psychologically damaging effect of frequent defeats at Munich Municipal golf course at the hands of a number of Jewish players, principally Sol Sternberg, Moshe Levinsky and Abe Horowitz.

Unflinchingly honest, my book examines in some detail Hitler's strong grip which caused him to hook the ball, especially off the tee, much to the amusement of Steinberg, Levinsky and Horowitz. Their laughter and Hitler's embarrassment fuelled a sense of grievance that led first to his giving up the game and then, by stages, to the Second World War and the Holocaust.

Among the many issues explored in the book is the role of Uwe Pretzel, the assistant pro at the Munich course. Had he, the book speculates, persuaded Hitler to move the thumb on his right hand further round the shaft thereby weakening the grip, maybe the Second World War would have been avoided and over 20 million lives spared.

Painstakingly researched, the book includes observations from, amongst others, Albert Speer, Field Marshall Rommel and Arnold Palmer. Particularly revealing are some comments made by former President Roosevelt, who notes how any reference to golf in the diplomatic exchanges with Hitler met with a frosty response.

Prime Minister Neville Chamberlain made the mistake of inviting Hitler to play in a fourball partnering Goering against himself and Lord Halifax at Wentworth. Hitler couldn't be tempted, not even when Chamberlain suggested Poland as a side-stake. When the Prime Minister accused the German Chancellor of being a 'scaredy-cat', Hitler went into a rage, slammed his putter onto the cabinet table and vowed to 'play through' Poland as if it were a 'single player with no standing'.

Would you be interested in publishing my book?

Dear Muirfield,

A very distant American cousin of mine, Marilyn Grossberger, has written to me eliciting my help in securing tee-times on your course. Obliged to assist but reluctant to become involved, I am merely forwarding you the relevant parts of her letter to me.

'I'm Chairperson of the Floridian Daughters of Elks, an alumni organization that helps keep graduates from the University of Florida, who were in the Elks' sorority, in touch with one another.

Every year we take a trip overseas (no husband or boyfriends allowed) and always have a real wild time. Last year about 50 of us went to Rio and had an absolute ball! This year about the same number will be coming to Bonny Scotland for a week at the end of July. So be prepared!

Based in Edinburgh, we'll be looking to do things that are both real fun and, where possible, sort of ethnic. I know that some of the girls would just love to play golf. A couple have played before but most would be giving it a whirl for the very first time. So what I'd like to know is:

1) Is it necessary to book or can we just turn up and go?

2) Can we rent sticks?

3) If we engage caddies, can we insist they wear kilts?

4) Is it extra to ride in those fun little cart things?

5) Should we wear special shoes or are normal, what I call 'shopping shoes', with short heels okay?

6) Can the women's locker room accommodate 50 players at one time? I mean, are their sufficient showers, mirrors, hair-dryers, etc.?

I'm really looking forward to knocking that silly little ball into that teeny-weeny ol' hole.'

I trust you will be able to help my cousin and I'm only sorry I won't be there to enjoy the spectacle.

Dear Prince Andrew,

First of all, thank you for the good work you're doing promoting golf. Too often the game is regarded by the general public as an elitist game that is the sole preserve of toffs, but you've done a great job demonstrating to the masses that everyone can play.

My purpose in writing is to ask you how a golf club goes about the business of having 'Royal' added to their name. I presume that someone royal like you has to come down, inspect the place and pass it as suitable for Royals generally. Is that right?

If there's an application form that has to be completed perhaps you would be kind enough to get one of your staff to post one to me.

The other thing of course is how much does it cost? Is there a one-off joining fee and then an annual subscription or what?

The people I've spoken to at my club are all agreed that it's a great idea and that it would considerably enhance our reputation, both in the area and nationally, as well as boost our green fee revenue thus helping to keep our subscriptions down.

By the way, if you were able to help us, we would be both honoured and privileged to offer you free lifetime membership, a club tie and possibly a reserved space in the car park. Can you imagine how good it would look if there was a sign that read: 'Reserved for HRH The Duke of York'? That should be worth a couple of quid on the green fee, eh?

Now that you're not opening fetes, visiting hospitals, dishing out medals and all that nonsense, presumably you've got plenty of time to work on your swing. And you might like to know there's a couple of cracking young girls working in the pro shop whom I'm sure you're going to like.

Dear Supreme Leader of North Korea (or can I call you Kim?),

When you were growing up, wasn't it a bit confusing having the same first name as your father? If your mother shouted, 'Kim, would you keep the noise down as I'm trying to watch television?' would you immediately know whom she was addressing? And that hyphen in your surname is rather exotic.

Here in the UK, it used to be that only the aristocracy had hyphens, but nowadays it seems more prevalent among black footballers than it is among toffs.

Anyway, I'm writing to you about a subject that I know is close to your heart – world peace. Like you, I'm a great believer in it and think I have found a way to turn it from a dream into reality. From my experience of playing golf for more than 40 years, I appreciate what a great opportunity it presents to make new friends and discuss things in a relaxed and calm environment.

Your dad, of course, was evidently a natural at the game and shot the proverbial lights out in the first round he ever played. Even if the six holes in one is possibly a slight exaggeration and, for argument's sake, he only had five, it's still sensational stuff. Thirty-eight under par is, quite frankly, incredible scoring.

My idea is for you to host a huge golf tournament (The Kim Classic?) on the Pyongyang course. Apart from anything else, an event such as this will help promote North Korea as a holiday destination. Instead of pros, you could invite world leaders to participate, nearly all of whom play golf, albeit not as well as your old man.

I would suggest a maximum of 72 players, a Stableford format (which should speed up play) and a complimentary bar. To mix things up a bit and reduce the risk of inadvertently aggravating an old border dispute, you could endeavour to go for a geographical spread and put, for example, a European prime minister in with an African tribal chief, a South American dictator and an Asian despot.

Selling the valuable TV rights to, say, Amazon Prime should generate sufficient revenue to pay for at least half-a-dozen medium-range rockets.

Dear Royal St George's

Having always wanted to be a film producer, I am very excited at the prospect of finally making a movie. The funding is in place and, having considered several possibly suitable locations, I would very much like to use your famous clubhouse and course for a film that is presently in what is called the 'development stage'. At the moment, we're working on a script and preparing budgets and I'm hoping that you might be willing to help.

To be absolutely honest with you, the film is not the sort you're likely to see at your local cinema. But there again that sort doesn't often make money. Ours is what is popularly termed an 'adult movie' and distribution will be by mail order and through specialised outlets only.

With the working title *'Confessions of a Golf Pro'*, it tells the story of a rather handsome golf professional who seduces his female pupils and most of the women's section at his club. He also employs two gorgeous Swedish assistants who keep the club members happy. As luck would have it, the pro-shop backs onto the men's showers, which makes life exciting for everyone.

The climax of the film, if that's a suitable term, comes when the golf pro is caught in bed with the captain's wife and the captain is similarly embarrassed when he's discovered in a bunker with one of the assistant pros by the club secretary, whose wife is next door having it away on the snooker table with the head greenkeeper.

Although there's a lot of sex and a fair bit of nudity, it's essentially a comedy that belongs somewhere in the *'Carry On'* tradition. Assuming you're happy for us to use your facilities – it would only be for three or four days in the summer – because budgets are necessarily tight, we would rather have some sort of contra deal than pay for the facility. In return for letting us use your clubhouse, I'm prepared to offer your members a unique opportunity to star in the film as extras and receive a complimentary DVD copy of it.

It might also be possible to hold the premiere at your club and invite all your members to attend. In view of the subject matter, it might be as well not to invite wives and girlfriends. Royal St George's will also be acknowledged in the film's end credits. For your information, the total crew including cameras, lighting, sound, makeup, director, actors and actresses should number no more than 30.

Are you 'up' for it?

Dear Jeremy Corbyn,

Although it's quite likely that you perceive golf as a rather bourgeois activity, nevertheless I sense you would welcome an opportunity to metaphorically smack a seven-iron against the backside of all Zionists, Israelis and Jews. Harold Wilson, one of your predecessors of course, was a very keen golfer and a member of Hampstead Golf Club, which is quite near your home in upmarket Islington. I believe he left the club in protest against their policy of not admitting Jews, which doubtless you would regard as something of a plus!

Even if you don't follow the game closely, you will have no doubt heard of the British Open Golf Championship, which has been going even longer than the Labour Party. But did you know that ever since the first Open was held in 1860, it has never been won by a Palestinian? And I think we all know who is to blame for that – yes, Israel of course.

Quite simply, very few Palestinians play golf because there are no courses for them to play on. Why, when the terrain, particularly around the sand dunes in Gaza, is ideally suited to golf? There's not even a nine-holer! Again, Israel is to blame because it has done absolutely nothing to encourage Palestinians to take up the game. What is Israel frightened of? That they will use the bunkers for military purposes? Or that they will thump long drives over the border fence without shouting 'fore' thereby threatening Israel's security?

Anti-semites throughout the UK are looking to you, Jeremy, to highlight the appalling apartheid that exists between golfers and non-golfers in the Middle East and, of course, to blame Israel for absolutely everything that's wrong in the world.

Dear League Against Cruel Sports,

I'm not sure if golf is on your list of cruel sports. If it isn't, it certainly should be.

It would be hard for me to overestimate the enormous amount of psychological damage that golf has inflicted on me. Formerly a calm and placid person, I'm now irritable and twitchy.

The unrelenting mental pressure starts on the first tee when you have to drive off in front of a whole load of strangers and doesn't stop until you've attempted to hole a testing six-foot downhill putt with a touch of left to right break to halve the match on the 18th.

Then there are all manner of other horrors that can strike at any time and are perfectly capable of reducing even the toughest of grown men to a gibbering wreck. I hate to even think it, let alone, type the dreaded word ... shank, aaaaaaaaaarrrrggggghhhhhhh!

If you don't play the game you will almost certainly be unfamiliar with the most awful shot in golf, which flies off the clubface at the most appalling of angles. The worst thing is that it can strike anyone at any time. And after it has happened once, you know that it can happen again. Consequently, every shot thereafter is an ordeal. And God forbid if it does happen again, then you're as good as dead.

And then there's putting and the dreaded yips... yeeeeeeeeeeeeeeeekkkkkkssssssss!

In case you don't know, the yips are an involuntary muscle spasm that twitches the putter head in your hand and causes you to miss comparatively short putts by embarrassingly huge distances. I've seen grown men reduced to tears and almost driven to suicide by this appalling affliction. As well as the psychological damage, golf can also ruin a perfectly good back and a perfectly good marriage.

Frankly foxhunting, hare coursing, and stag hunting, although somewhat messy, are comparatively benign activities. At least they only harm animals.

I'm planning a protest demonstration outside the main entrance at the next Open Championship. However many people you're able to send in support would be most welcome. And so please hurry up and add golf to your list of cruel sports.

Dear Pope,

Let me make myself clear from the outset, I'm not Roman Catholic. Apart from anything else, my dodgy hip makes it difficult for me to kneel, which would render praying rather problematic. And praying is clearly an important part of your religion. Not that I would be required to do anything about it unless I had ambitions to be a monk, celibacy is something else which, frankly, has little or no appeal.

Although, as I say, Catholicism doesn't grab me by the cassock, so to speak, I remain open-minded about religion generally and could possibly be persuaded to join your lot if it could be demonstrated to work. Doubtless that sounds a bit unreasonable to someone like you who obviously has enormous faith, but I'm a practical and pragmatic man who needs

He did, he just prayed to end a golfer's Yips problem...

concrete evidence that a thing works before I'm prepared to give up my Sunday mornings to sit on an uncomfortable bench in an absurdly spacious and draughty building. Those candles don't give off a great deal of heat, do they?

What, you might reasonably ask, is it that I do on a Sunday morning that's more important than saving my soul? Well, unless it's raining, I would ordinarily be playing golf at Dale Hill Hotel and Golf Club, which is just to the south-east of Tunbridge Wells. I don't know whether it's the close proximity of nature or just the sheer fun of it all but, curiously, I believe there is a spiritual aspect to golf that undoubtedly has a religious dimension, although not perhaps in a conventional way. How else do you explain my friend Harry's ridiculous hole-in-one where the ball hit two trees and a waste-paper bin on its way into the hole? Harry, who was 78, had been playing golf for over 50 years and never had a hole-in-one before, died two days later. At last he was at peace.

Now to the main point of my letter. My putting has completely gone to pieces. I shan't try and explain the 'yips' to someone who doesn't play golf and is too preoccupied looking after the welfare of an estimated 1.2 billion people to worry too much about a poor 19 handicapper for whom three-putting is an enormous source of anguish, but it's a nightmare. The club pro hasn't been much help and so, forgive me asking, but do you know of a prayer that could sort it out? Or do you think, say, dipping my putter head in holy water might do the trick? Last question; is there a patron saint of golfers to whom I could appeal or stick a replica of him on my golf bag?

If you are able to help and my handicap drops below, say, 15, I promise to convert.

Dear Ewen Murray,

Forgive me writing to you as I've no doubt you're being approached the whole time by people wanting you to play at their club, open fetes or support their charity. Well, I've got a proposal that I believe will make me rich and you even richer.

A good friend of mine, who is a nuclear physicist, has been helping me for the past four years develop a revolutionary putter that tests have confirmed is five times more likely to hole a putt than a conventional putter. Unbelievable but true.

His handicap has tumbled from 19 to 10 in the 12 months we've been testing our new Krypton putter. How has he improved so much? Look at the stats. He's hitting no more fairways than before (averaging 3.2 a round), reaching no more greens in regulation (2.8 a round) or registering more sand saves (lifetime average seemingly stuck on 0.27%) but he now regularly takes fewer than 23 putts a round (his record is an astonishing 19!).

Working at a Ministry of Defence research laboratory gives him access to material and facilities denied to civilians. Anyway, all conventional putters are primarily focused on good balance. You might be surprised to learn that the Krypton putter isn't. All it does is literally impart a massive positive charge that effectively magnetises the ball so when it approaches or passes near the hole, it is attracted to the negative charge in the metal of the cup and is pulled towards it until it inevitably disappears into it.

Field tests have highlighted just a couple of minor problems that I feel obliged to disclose to you. Firstly, as it has an even stronger electrostatic field than the cup, the flagstick has to be removed well away otherwise the ball may adhere to it and be virtually impossible to remove. Secondly, there is a slight health and safety issue due to the depleted uranium core that is in the putter head. However, using a putter-cover impregnated with copper and a lead-lined golf bag, significantly reduces radiation levels. Mind you, finding a caddy who can lift a 225-pound golf bag can be a challenge.

In return for a modest percentage of the profits, would you be willing to endorse the Krypton and mention it on Sky every time you get the chance?

○○○○○

Dear St Andrews,

Although you're doubtless disappointed that the Open Championship won't be coming to your course for a few years at least, you should perhaps be grateful, as it will give you an opportunity to carry out the improvements detailed below.

St Andrews is undoubtedly steeped in history, but what strikes me most of all whenever I watch golf being played there on TV is how featureless it is compared to the great American courses like Augusta National and Pebble Beach. Frankly, it's rather dull and so what can be done to improve it? It came to me like a well-struck seven-iron. What's the most important hole on a golf course? Why, the 18th of course, the finishing hole. So, perversely, this is where I suggest you start.

At the moment it's a rather uninteresting, short, par four. Goodness me, it's almost driveable! The Swilken Burn doesn't present enough of a hazard to worry the better players and, let's face it, most of the guys teeing it up at the British Open are more than averagely good. So what you must do is dam up the Swilken Burn and let the water flood the surrounding area until you've got a decent lake. It's a shame that the pretty stone bridge will be lost but you can always find an alternative spot to stick it somewhere on the course. Or you might prefer to flog it to some rich Yank such as Donald Trump and the proceeds would help pay for the landscaping.

A nice big lake would make the competitors think more carefully on the tee. The trouble with the hole at present is that nothing very exciting ever happens apart from some poor geezer missing a short putt.

To top it all off tastefully and provide some visual interest, I suggest you install a really big fountain. A statue in the middle of, say, an old man stooped under the weight of his golf bag could be very effective, especially if there were jets of water streaming out of his clubs and into the sky. And a few Koi carp in the lake wouldn't do any harm either. They're not cheap but if you can persuade visitors that their golfing luck will improve if they empty their pockets into it, both the fish and the lake will have paid for themselves in no time.

The St Andrews fountain could become the most famous fountain in the whole of golf, which you might care to use for branding identity purposes on your merchandise.

Since I've probably given you enough to think about for now, I'll leave my idea on how to divide those ridiculous double greens with the careful use of Leylandii hedging for another time.

Dear Dr Ping,

You will be thrilled to learn that I have one of your putters. I got it cheap on eBay but am delighted with it. Every so often it seems to miss a bit on the right-hand side but, to be honest, it could very well be my fault and not the putter's.

I'm writing because I've had what I think is a very good idea and would be interested to hear what you think of it. To take advantage of the twilight rate at my local course, I frequently tee off in the early evening. The place is blissfully quiet and the only downside is the light frequently fails towards the end of the round. Because I don't drive the ball very far, the poor visibility is less of a problem on the tee than it is on the green. I find reading the line of the putts increasingly difficult as the sun sinks while my putts don't. But, rather than moan, I've done something about it.

It's very simple really as it's essentially nothing much more than a torch that can be easily attached to the shaft of the putter. To distribute the weight more evenly, I've located the battery in the grip with a wire going down the interior of the shaft. Incidentally, the same battery supplies power to a small coil heater that keeps the grip warm on a cold evening.

The torch is adjustable, as is the beam, so that I can illuminate a specific spot either on the line of the putt or on the hole itself. As a courtesy to my opponents, I always turn it off when they're putting. It really works incredibly well and the only negative is that it attracts annoying moths that can be an unwanted distraction and so I'm presently developing a device that emits a high-pitched screech that I'm hoping will scare them off.

My idea is to sell the kit that would enable golfers to convert their existing putters. All customers would need is a power drill, soldering iron and rudimentary knowledge of applied electro-physics. I'm hoping you will be willing to endorse my product along the lines of: *As recommended by Dr Ping.*

Dear Head of Bombing 48th Fighter Wing, RAF,

I'm considering building a brand-new golf course and have an option to purchase what is presently a sheep farm on Romney Marsh, Kent. However, I'll need some help and that is why I'm writing to you.

The 150-acre farm is ideal for golf in every respect other than it is almost completely flat. Although flatness might be a significant advantage in an airfield, it is quite definitely a disadvantage in a golf course.

I've looked at the landscaping option and, frankly, it is simply too costly to move hundreds of tons of earth about.

It was whilst watching 'Apocalypse Now' that the idea came to me. Presumably you are always looking for new areas on which to practise your bombing. So, how about dropping a few cluster bombs and daisy cutters on my proposed golf course? Although it would be nice if they could be precisely targeted to create, for example, suitable greenside bunkers, frankly, it wouldn't matter too much where they landed, provided of course that they didn't stray onto the nearby housing estate or main road, as collateral damage is probably best avoided.

In return for your help, I'm happy to offer the pilots who actually drop the bombs complimentary membership of my club and all other USAF and RAF personnel, 50 per cent off the usual green fee.

Dear GCSE Examination Board,

I'm encouraged that modern education extends beyond the three R's and that children are leaving school with a broader understanding of the world. However, there is one vital area of human activity that is still largely being ignored… golf.

I believe the Royal and Ancient game is a legitimate area of study and should be included in the national curriculum. So, in a bid to start the ball rolling, so to speak, I've drafted a dummy GCSE level golf examination paper that will give you a good idea of what I'm about. Perhaps have a go at it yourself and let me know what you think.

Golf (Theory) GCSE Examination.

Although this paper should take no more than three-and-a-half hours to complete, it will probably take longer.

Candidates should be aware that if they fall more than one question behind the candidate in front of them, they should call through whoever is sitting behind.

Write an essay on one of the following:

1. Ben Hogan has a better swing than Nick Faldo, but the Englishman wore more interesting sweaters. Discuss.

or

Was what happened in the Ryder Cup at Brooklyn, Massachusetts, an indictment of matchplay golf or simply a few boozed-up Yanks misbehaving themselves?

or

Golfers have no dress sense. Discuss

2. Match up the golfers in column A with the most appropriate description in column B.

A)	B)
Tommy Fleetwood	God-fearing
Bernard Langer	Pissed
Bryson DeChambeau	Phenomenally rich
Shane Lowry	A Nutter
Tiger Woods	Needs a haircut
Nick Faldo	Should go on a diet
John Daly	Not very popular

3. Your ball lands in a cowpat. Do you
   a) Claim relief, on the basis that playing it as it lies is just too disgusting?
   b) Nudge it away gently with your shoe when your playing partners aren't looking? *or*
   c) Drop it within two clubs' length under penalty of one stroke?

4. A member of your regular fourball never buys a round of drinks. Without recourse to physical violence, explain how you would deal with the situation.

5. Which is the odd one out and why?

   St Andrews, Royal Troon, Carnoustie, Royal Birkdale, Royal St. George's and Dale Hill Hotel and Golf Club

6. Your club car park is full except for the space reserved for the captain. Do you:

   a) Find somewhere else to park? *or*

   b) Reverse into the Captain's spot and accidentally knock down the sign so that you can claim that you didn't realize it was his? *or*

   c) Park alongside the 18th green by way of protest at the inadequate parking provision and be prepared to join another club?

7. Using diagrams, explain what happens when you shank a ball.

Dear British Psychiatric Association,

I presume you keep a central register of all known psychiatric disorders, which your members can refer to when trying to figure out what afflicts their patients. Well, if you would allow me, I would like to add one which I doubt you will have come across because it's a niche condition that only afflicts a small but hugely important sector of society – golfers.

Broadly speaking it's a neurotic reluctance to use a new golf ball. To save you the bother of dreaming up a clever name for it, I've already thought of one: novospherophobia. A long-time sufferer, I hope that by 'coming out' and drawing attention to the condition I might help others and remove some of the stigma attached to it.

Thanks to friends and family, whose generosity outweighs their originality at Christmas and on my birthday, I have boxes of shiny new golf balls on the top of my wardrobe next to my Spurs' DVDs. To those who know me, golf balls must seem an ideal gift. After all, doesn't Mortimer just love golf? Well, yes, but much as I love golf, I hate using a new ball. Why?

It's a complicated business. One explanation is that I'm an anal retentive who likes to hoard. Although there's no history of stamps or cheese labels, I'm reluctant to throw things away and have an absolute hang-up about waste. Or maybe it's connected with my profound insecurity and I subconsciously measure my own worth in new Titleists and Pinnacles. It's not that I especially like new golf balls, I just simply hate to use them.

Why won't I use them? One reason is that I have a firm belief that new balls are not very different from old balls. A scratch here, a scuff there doesn't, in my opinion, significantly affect their aerodynamic properties. In other words, struck properly, old balls fly just as straight and are no more likely to end up in trouble if they're not.

The real reason I believe I can't bring myself to take a virgin ball out of its box and tee it up is that I don't want the added pressure. Golf is a worrying game at the best of times without the extra anxiety that comes from using a new ball. If, in a moment of extreme carelessness, I inadvertently teed one up and, God forbid, hit it into deep rough, I would feel obliged to look for it for the full three minutes. Then, if I didn't find it, I'd be inconsolable for the rest of the round and, depending on the light, might even return to the spot later to resume the search.

So under what circumstances, if any, would I break into my war chest of literally dozens of new balls? That's a tough question. Clearly, if I were to make it through the qualifiers and find myself on the first tee at The Open, it would be just too embarrassing to declare to the likes of Tiger and Rory as I pulled a ball at random out of my golf bag, 'Mine's a weary looking Top Flite number two with a scratchy mark running down one side and an odd-looking logo on the other.'

But if I were obliged to start with a new ball, I would hope to finish the round with the same one, tee it up the next day and, assuming I made the cut, play the final two rounds with it as well. Moreover, I doubt very much that, even after four rounds, I would feel inclined to toss it nonchalantly into the crowd as I walked off the 18th green.

Taking out a new ball every couple of holes, as the pros do, is profligate nonsense. I suspect this practice is the consequence of collusion between the manufacturers, eager to dump surplus stock in an effort to maintain prices, and the caddies, looking to supplement their modest wages by flogging nearly-new golf balls on the side.

Although not strictly a qualified psychiatrist, I have devised a highly effective treatment and am presently organising some weekend clinics in conjunction with Dale Hill Hotel and Golf Club, the details of which I'm hoping you might circulate amongst your members so that they can refer desperate sufferers directly to me.

On the first morning patients are taken by minibus to nearby Bewl Water, which is an 800-acre reservoir and the largest stretch of open water in the south-east of England. Here they are asked to try and drive brand new balls over the reservoir, a carry of just over a mile. Initially they struggle to take the club back, their palms grow sweaty and they frequently weep uncontrollably as each despairing shot splashes into the water.

However, as the treatment progresses, they learn to relax and actually appear to enjoy the experience. A cure is considered to have been effected when they dispense with their drivers and start hitting wedge shots in a carefree way that betrays obvious pleasure. At £995 + VAT, the treatment in not cheap but sufferers have nothing to lose except, of course, their balls.

Dear Challenge Tour,

As the significantly inferior of the two main European tours, I think yours would be the ideal place to introduce an experimental leaderboard that I'm hoping will eventually come to be regarded as just as important as the existing Order of Merit.

You see, I think there is a real danger that you're taking this competitive thing just a wee bit too seriously. In constantly rewarding and glorifying the winners, I fear you are guilty of ignoring the non-winners who, for whatever reason and not necessarily through any fault of their own, don't finish on top. In the modern era, this kind of discrimination between those with exceptional talent and those without it, is no longer acceptable.

You would do well to follow the example of Miss Charlotte Flowers, who was my primary school teacher. In many ways she was very many years ahead of her time. With the help of a complicated formula that frankly none of us understood, she calculated who in the class had effectively over-achieved the most and gave him or her a prize.

You could do the same and run a sort of Triers Leaderboard in parallel with the Order of Merit that rewarded such qualities as effort and determination; and virtues such as kindness and consideration for others. In that way you would demonstrate that golf was genuinely inclusive of those who were perfectly adequate players but not exceptional and that shooting low scores was not the only thing that mattered.

Compared with simply counting the number of shots, assessing how hard someone is trying or how considerate of others they are, is much more difficult. The best way, in my opinion, is to ask the playing partners to submit 'Behaviour' scorecards after the round. For example: did your playing partner put you off at all, step on your line, fidget while you were playing your shot, congratulate you when you hit a long drive and commiserate with you when you missed a putt? In this way we would discover who are the genuinely nice guys, which is something I sincerely believe fans are keen to know.

I won't insist but it would be a nice touch if you called what I'm proposing, 'The Charlotte Flowers Leaderboard'.

Dear Mr Callaway,

Golf equipment is, I know, a very competitive business. Because the only thing that matters to the overwhelming majority of golfers is smashing the ball further, this rivalry must be particularly acute when it comes to drivers. Irons are all very well and wedges certainly have their place but I suspect the driver is the flagship in your fleet. If you can outgun the opposition, then you're well on the way to the top of the pile and I'm certain I can help you achieve that.

Ever since I was a young lad, I've been interested in explosives. As a boy, I would take fireworks apart and then put them back together so that they behaved differently to the way the manufacturers intended. I would change the colours around, make rockets fly further and increase the decibel level of the bangs. This background in explosives has helped me in my recent quest to develop a driver that will really hit the ball immense distances, and I mean IMMENSE.

You'll understand, I know, that for commercial reasons I'm not in a position to reveal the details but I have developed a club I call the 'Howitzer' that consistently hits the ball comfortably over 400 yards. My record to date on flat terrain with no following wind is 518 yards. Imagine driving the green on a par five! And the best thing about it is that anyone can achieve these distances because club head speed is almost totally irrelevant.

As with all new technology there are one or two teething problems. The principal headache, and I choose the word advisedly, that I'm wrestling with at the moment is the almost unbearable noise. Unsurprisingly, the club at impact sounds not unlike a very loud shotgun, which can be quite a problem when, as is often the case, the tee is adjacent to a green that may or may not have people putting on it.

The other challenge is trying to eliminate the near blinding flash that accompanies the bang. During trials, I've been wearing goggles and ear-muffs and there is clearly a commercial opportunity in selling these accessories along with the

'Howitzer'. Because there are so many conservative elements in the golfing establishment, I would be lying if I said everyone will welcome the 'Howitzer'. But you have experience of these and doubtless an expert legal department that will help you overcome these reactionary elements.

In conclusion, what I'm hoping for is some form of joint venture with you that married my technical genius with your considerable experience to our great mutual advantage.

Dear Brother or Sister Chairperson of the Communist Party of Great Britain,

The last couple of decades have been pretty depressing for those of us who have been eagerly anticipating the imminent collapse of capitalism and the long-awaited takeover by the oppressed proletariat. On the other hand, the weather seems to be steadily improving and Spurs are still in the Premiership.

Although I'm completely confident that brother Karl more or less got it right when he predicted the inevitable demise of capitalism, I believe that the irresistible forces of history might need to be gently encouraged if this particular working-class hero is to be around to witness the revolution.

Somewhat weary of working within the system to bring about its collapse (I had a temporary job at my local newsagent and deliberately creased copies of the *Daily Telegraph*) I now recognise that there is no alternative to direct action. I believe the time is right to strike at the soft underbelly of capitalism and hit the exploiters where they gather in great numbers to orchestrate their oppression. I'm referring, of course, to golf clubs.

Although destroying all the clubhouses has considerable appeal, a more subtle approach might be less confrontational.

What I propose, therefore, is that we metaphorically tear down the symbols of power by moving to a distant corner of the car park all the spaces reserved for the Chairmen, Captains and Lady Captains. Apart from the enormous psychological impact to be gained from striking at the undemocratic symbols of elitism and power, the practical chaos that will be wrought when BMW, Mercedes, and other flash motors are ousted from their regular spaces, will almost certainly throw the oppressors into disarray. At that moment, while they are all looking for somewhere to park, we'll move in and seize control of the means of production, the media and whatever else we need in order to liberate the masses.

Dear Chairman of the International Olympic Committee,

The Olympics are fast becoming one of the undoubted highlights of the sporting calendar, spanning so many different sports and involving so many athletes. It's too bad the winter Olympics have to take place in the winter but I don't suppose there is anything you can do about that. Anyway, the summer Olympics are unbelievably popular and have a global appeal that's right up there with the University Boat Race and Greyhound Derby.

However, as you know better than most it's fatal to become complacent and the Olympics must continually evolve if they are to maintain their pre-eminence. And so it was that I began thinking what I could do to improve things. Because of a personal worry I have about energy conservation and global warming, I wonder sometimes about the example being set by having the Olympic flame burning so extravagantly the whole time. I appreciate its symbolic importance but feel that it could at least be reduced in size or, better still, switched off between events. Another thing, is anyone really interested in dressage or synchronized swimming?

I'm so pleased you finally caved in to financial pressure from the likes of Nike, Titleist and Ping and reinstated golf. However, do we really need yet another 72-hole, strokeplay tournament that is hardly distinguishable from any other golf event?

So here's what I suggest. Each country that wishes to participate should enter a fourball team made up of a professional golfer, a businessman, a showbiz celebrity and a prominent politician. The US dream team, for example, could be made up of Tiger Woods, Bill Gates, Jack Nicholson and Donald Trump. Imagine both the enormous interest that would be generated and the opportunities it will create for world leaders to sort out their problems in a relaxed atmosphere over a pint of beer in the clubhouse afterwards.

The two best balls of the four to count and, because I don't doubt whether the celebrities and politicians have the stamina, it probably should be an 18-hole event.

Dear Messrs Royal and Ancient,

First of all may I congratulate you on a wonderful game. I took up golf over 50 years ago and, in my humble opinion, it's better than darts, snooker and bowls put together. Although quite what a game made up of a combination of those three would look like and what sort of scoring system there would be is somewhat hard to imagine but I hope you get my point.

Anyway, my purpose in writing is to offer a few suggestions as to how the game might be improved. Even with the reduction in the time allowed to look for balls, too many minutes are wasted thrashing around impenetrable undergrowth. Why? Because the 'shot and distance' rule is far too harsh. Instead, I think a player who has either lost a ball or can't be arsed to look for it should be allowed to drop another one more or less where he was aiming the original ball at the cost of just one shot.

Also, escaping from bunkers is far too difficult for the ordinary man or woman, especially when the ball is in an awkward spot. Without penalty, I suggest a player be allowed to kick the ball just once in a bunker to a more reasonable position provided that it remains on the sand and in the bunker.

Where a player accidentally hits a ball out of bounds but there was no intent on his part to secure an advantage by, say, cutting a corner, he may play the shot again with no penalty. Since golf is an honourable game played by honourable men and women, the final decision as to whether there was intent or not rests solely with the player.

Finally, to make putting both more exciting and fairer, a putt that lips out should count as one-and-a-half shots but the putt should be deemed to have been holed. For example, a player putting for a four whose ball lips out should score four-and-a-half not five. In matchplay, obviously four-and-a-half beats a five but in strokeplay all half shots are rounded up at the end to avoid awkward scores such as 104-and-a-half, which of course would count as 105.

$$\bigcirc\bigcirc\bigcirc\bigcirc\bigcirc$$

Dear Acushnet,

Although I don't buy any, I'm always pleased if I find a Titleist so your advertising clearly works, even if it doesn't always necessarily result in increased sales. And it's about the issue of lost golf balls that I'm writing to you.

As an environmentalist, I'm rather concerned that they are polluting the planet. It's not your fault because it's not you who are losing them. However, as the manufacturer, I believe you have a social responsibility here. My worry is that your balls contain a number of toxic substances that contaminate both the soil and water, thereby harming mammals, fish, birds and even often-forgotten insects.

Instead of simply complaining, I have come up with an environmentally friendly alternative. Called the Ecoball, it's made entirely of vegetable matter – mostly a blend of crushed walnut shells and shredded acorns. It's non-toxic and biodegradable.

Lost Ecoballs simply rot and, far from doing damage, actually enrich the soil. My research also shows that they are positively liked by certain species of fish, particularly carp, which eagerly feed on the decaying matter.

In a world of increasing environmental awareness I believe that there are a growing number of people, and golfers are not very different from ordinary people, who would willingly pay a small premium for a product that was environmentally benign.

The only significant drawbacks I've so far encountered with the Ecoball are: 1) Their tendency to dissolve in water renders them impractical in wet weather; 2) You can't leave them too long on a damp fairway whilst, for example, looking for your playing partner's ball, because they will start to take root; and 3) They travel a little under half the distance of a conventional ball. Regarding the last point, I believe responsible golfers would willingly trade a little length in return for not harming the planet, don't you?

Would you be interested in some form of joint venture, which combined your manufacturing and marketing might with my pioneering concept?

Dear William Hill,

Not since Oxo won the Grand National quite a few years ago have I had a bet. However, I fancy a tickle on a forthcoming competition at Dale Hill Hotel and Golf Club, which is where I've been a member since 1986 but still haven't been invited to be club captain. Perhaps you can give me odds on that happening before I move on up to the Great Clubhouse in the Sky. Another time, perhaps.

The July Mid-Week Stableford is the competition I have in mind. It normally attracts a modest field that barely reaches double figures but that need not concern you as the somewhat complicated bet I have in mind has nothing do with the result.

As usual, I shall be playing with the same group I've played with every week for the past 27 years – Martin, Peter and Guy. I appreciate that I ought to make a greater effort to get to know more of the members but somehow can't be arsed. To be honest, although Guy's okay, the other two are incredibly dull. Martin moans the whole time about his arthritic hip while Peter has to be among the slowest golfers on the planet.

Anyway, I would like an accumulator on the following. To make it easier for you since you obviously don't know the people involved, I have inserted what I honestly consider are fair approximate odds next to each leg of the bet. If you would like to conduct further research, I can let you have the mobile phone numbers of the other three so that you can chat to them and make up your own mind.

Martin being the last to turn up	5/4
Guy forgetting a pencil to mark the card	1/1
My drive down the first being the longest in our group	2/1
Me hitting the green on all four par threes	4/1
Me not going into any bunker the entire round	5/2
Me not three-putting at all	4/1
Guy hitting at least one T-shot out of bounds	4/6
Martin uttering at least two audible expletives on each nine	1/1
Peter losing at least one ball on each nine	4/5
My nett score being the lowest	11/4
Peter offering to buy the first round of drinks	7/4

By my reckoning, but I think you should do your own calculation, the cumulative odds of all the above happening are 65,780 to one. If so, I should like to put the enclosed fiver on, please, to win £328,904.

Finally, I noted in a recent promotion of yours that you were offering to return punters' stakes in the event of one leg of an accumulator going down. Is that still valid? In which case, if only 10 of the above 11 come good, do I get my fiver back?

Dear Rishi Sunak,

I don't know whether or not you play golf but, either way, I'm certain you are going to like the incredible idea I've had.

It came to me when riding upstairs on the 88 bus travelling along the Bayswater Road. Looking out at the enormous expanse of grass that is Hyde Park, it surprised me how few people there were enjoying this excellent facility. Then it struck me; what a wonderful opportunity exists for developing a truly, world-beating golf course right in the centre of the world's greatest city.

So excited was I by the idea that I immediately jumped off the bus and took a good look around. And the more I looked, the more excited I became. For example, the Serpentine could, with a little imagination and re-shaping, make a wonderful water feature guarding the green of a tricky par three.

Although I appreciate there are a few royals knocking about in Kensington Palace, I'm sure they wouldn't mind being confined to, say, the top floor to enable the balance of the building to be converted into arguably the greatest and most historic clubhouse in the world. Possibly the only negative I can detect in the whole scheme is that there's no way to avoid felling a few old trees. But I would estimate no more than four or five hundred would need to go.

The big plus from both your and the Treasury's point of view would be the enormous income that would be generated. At present there's just the deckchair rental and a modest revenue from the Serpentine café but I'm talking tens of millions of pounds. Membership of the incredibly exclusive Royal Hyde Park Golf and Country Club (Patron: HM the King) would be hugely sought-after by all those fat cats who live in Kensington, Belgravia and Knightsbridge. Even at half-a-million quid, I'm certain you would have no difficulty enrolling, say, 1000 members.

Then there are the corporates! How much do you think a Japanese bank would pay to join? Five million? The revenue would be fantastic and we've not even considered bar sales and the pro shop. And what about the worldwide merchandising possibilities? The income could help to make good Boris's extravagant election promise to boost the NHS and leave enough left over to fund a significant tax cut in the next budget to satisfy your rich friends. Handled properly and provided your daft Brexit doesn't bugger everything up, it could on its own almost guarantee you another few years in the top job.

Dear Wentworth,

'GLOVE' was formed three years ago. The letters are an acronym for 'Growing Lovely Organic Vegetables Everywhere'. Appropriately, for all gloves, but obviously not mittens, have five fingers, we have adopted a five-point programme to help combat the world food shortage whilst not harming our delicate environment.

The first of the five points is, 'To identify suitable sites for planting, growing and harvesting vegetables.' These sites can be anything from railway embankments and motorway verges to waste tips and roundabouts. They literally come in all shapes and sizes. What they all have in common is that they are otherwise unproductive. At our recent AGM, one of our Surrey members came up with the enormously interesting suggestion that we investigate the possibilities that exist on golf courses. She lives quite close to you and thought you might be willing to help.

From my own extensive experience of golf, I know that there are substantial tracts of land within the boundaries of the course that, for all practical purposes, are redundant. These unproductive stretches are the ones that we will first identify and then develop sensitively.

This is how GLOVE works. One of our people will 'recce' your land, identify suitable areas and conduct soil tests. We will then draw up a planting programme tailor-made for you. What we call our farmhands are trained to be unobtrusive but, so that you can readily identify them, they wear bright yellow overalls with a big red glove logo on the back. Anyway, they will prepare the soil, sow the seeds, tend the plants and harvest the crop.

Our determined aim is to cause you as little disturbance as possible. Indeed, you will hardly have to do anything. All we ask is that you desist from using any insecticides, weed-killers, fungicides or any other chemical treatment within 800 yards of our plots. We would also very much appreciate it if, when you mow the fairways and greens, that you pile the clippings onto a convenient compost heap. If any of your members want to help they could, when passing the heap, stuff some compost into their golf bags and then spread it on any plots they happen to pass during their round.

In return for all your help, we are happy to give your club 10% of everything we grow on your course. Should you want more, we'll gladly sell it to you at a generous 25% discount on our normal prices.

Dear British Museum (Early Man Department)

You may or may not be aware that there is some confusion and dispute about the origins of golf and in which country it was first played. The Scots would have you believe that they invented it, as would the Dutch, American Indians, Mongols, Greeks and many others. Considerable national prestige is the prize to be won by the country that can prove that it's the only true originator of the game.

All the above leads me on to a rather extraordinary find I made last month whilst playing in my club's midweek Stableford. Rather uncharacteristically for me, since I tend to draw the ball rather than fade it, I sliced my drive into the trees on the right side of the par four 14th. My suspicion is that I probably took the club back outside the line and failed to bring it back to square on impact. Since the ball was a pretty decent one, I ventured into the woods in search of it. Although I never in fact found it, what I did discover was indeed quite remarkable.

First of all, there was a very old bone that had been fashioned into something akin to a lob wedge. There will, I know, be sceptics who will say that it is just an old bone that happens to resemble the shape of a golf club. However, close inspection of the top of the bone reveals heavy scratch marks.

The significance of these is quite clear to me. If indeed what I found was an early, say Neolithic golf club, it would have been used during a particularly wet period in the earth's history. Heavy rain will have rendered the club slippery and early man, without the benefit of modern all-weather grips, will have needed to improve adhesion by effectively roughing up the top of the club. This will have given him a competitive edge and, who knows, improved his chances of capturing the Club Championship and mating with whoever he chose from the women's section.

Before you dismiss this as pure speculation, you should examine the 'ball' I found nearby. Although considerably heavier and with far fewer dimples than the modern equivalent and almost certainly less responsive around the green, it would undoubtedly have done the job.

It occurred to me that an ancient predecessor of mine might have entered the self-same wood, searching for his ball, some several thousand years earlier and been attacked by a sabre-toothed tiger.

Given the likely historical significance, I'm reluctant to post the objects. Would it be possible to bring them along and show them to an expert?

Dear American Golf,

Before I introduce you to my amazing invention, may I ask whose side are you on in the Ryder Cup? Your name suggests you support the Yanks. Is that right?

Never mind, my purpose in writing to you now is to introduce you to the incredible Pentapole which, as the name suggests, is five things in one; all of which every golfer should take with him or her onto the course.

Okay, you've hit your opening tee shot into a fairway bunker. After you've knocked it back on the fairway, there's a problem… no rake. Don't panic, simply pick up your Pentapole, flick the control to 'R' and out will pop a rake with a reach of just over two metres. Finished with it? Simply press 'R' again and the rake will withdraw back into the Pentapole.

As you wedge-it to the green, you take a significant divot which flies 10 feet in front of you. You don't have to walk forward to pick it up and back to replace it, just flick the switch on your Pentapole to 'D' and a five-pronged, metal 'hand' will extend up to three metres, scoop up the divot and return it to you. Incidentally, the divot returner doubles as a ball retriever to recover wayward shots that, for example, plop into a water hazard or on the wrong side of a barbed-wire fence.

Your next tee shot lands three-quarters of the way up a hill and leaves you with a blind shot to the green. Is there anyone on the green? And where on the green is the flag? Don't trudge up the hill to look, just press 'P' on your Pentapole and an eight-metre long periscope will extend upwards to give you a clear sight of the green.

Now you're on the green and worried that the group behind, because they can't see you, might hit up and cause you injury at best and miss the putt at worst. Press 'F' on the Pentapole control and the periscope will once again rise eight metres in the air but this time a red flag will spring out while a high-pitched alarm will sound so you will be both visible and audible to the group behind.

Finally, as you stride up the 18th, a threatening cloud looms up behind the clubhouse. Could it be a thunderstorm? Don't panic, just press 'L' on your Pentapole control and a 15-metre lightning conductor will soar skyward. Plant it in the ground and then stroll to the clubhouse knowing that any lightning in the vicinity will strike it and not you.

Final point, don't forget to go back out and retrieve your Pentapole before driving home as they cost £99.99. Cheap for an item that saves you money and energy while protecting you from being struck both by other golfers and God. How many Pentapoles would you like to order for your shops?

Dear Armitage Shanks,

Like many with a handicap as high as mine, I get rather nervous before commencing a round of golf and almost invariably have to visit the gents. That in itself is not a problem but for the fact that your toiletware (is that the correct word?), which in all other respects is fine, causes me considerable anguish simply because of the name, 'Armitage Shanks', which is displayed quite prominently on the urinals, doubtless for marketing purposes. I tried switching to the cubicles but there it was again on the toilet bowls. There really is no escaping it.

I have no problem with 'Armitage', which is indeed an elegant name, but 'Shanks' is very problematic for those, like me, who have an unhappy history of occasionally hitting golf balls almost sideways. In the UK we call that unmentionable shot a – I can hardly bring myself to type the word – shank … aaaarrrrgggggghhhh!. It's horrible and incredibly destructive. It got so bad with me that I paid a fortune to see a sports psychologist who said I must obliterate all thoughts of it from my mind. How can I do that when your company's name screams out at me before I have even walked to the first tee? There are some bushes at the back of the car park but, although there's nothing in the Rules of Golf about it, old-fashioned golf clubs, and mine is one of those, frown on that sort of thing; if caught I could be suspended or even thrown out.

May I therefore respectfully urge you to re-brand your products in the UK? Having given it considerable thought, I believe I have an altogether better and more acceptable name. 'Flush' is a good positive word in golf that means to strike the ball perfectly. And, of course, it's appropriate to your industry. And so 'Armitage Flush' would ensure continuity whilst at the same time avoiding distressing anxious golfers like me.

Dear St Andrews Golf Museum

Because it was raining so heavily when I visited St Andrews in February (unusual for Scotland, eh?), I wasn't able to achieve my life's ambition of playing the Old Course and so I instead wandered around your museum. Although quite interesting, it was no substitute for the Road Hole or taking on the Swilken Burn. Never mind. Anyway, I have an idea for 'beefing' up your exhibits which I'm hoping you will like.

Next month I'm having my left hip replaced, which set me thinking. I have very little idea of what my left hip or, for that matter, my right hip, looks like. The same is true of the rest of my joints and all my internal organs. Since the purpose of museums is to educate and entertain, don't you think it would add enormously to the appeal of yours if you could display body parts in an attractive and interesting way?

Although I've not formally asked, I've no doubt the Conquest Hospital in Hastings would be happy to post you my old hip.

However, I recognise that, despite the fact that I'm still the only member at Dale Hill Hotel and Golf Club to have won three consecutive monthly mid-week Stableford competitions (1976 – September, October and November), my hip isn't of huge interest to many people. The same, I don't think, could be said of, say, Jon Daly's liver or Tiger Woods's back.

In the same way that we're all being asked to carry organ donor cards, perhaps you could persuade the top players to do something similar so, in the event of their death, you would have first dibs on their body parts. It may sound a bit grisly but it would be very educational.

Dear Sotheby's,

I guess that you hold regular auctions and therefore should be in a good position to advise me what I should do with my tee pegs. If you don't play golf, you might not know that tee-pegs are the little structures upon which you place your ball when driving off.

Ever since I started playing golf back in the early 1970s I've collected them. Today I have somewhere in the region of 25,000.

My collection is held in over 100 shoe boxes and is filed according to material: 'wood', 'plastic', and 'other': by height: 'very tall', 'tall', 'moderately tall', 'average', 'below average', 'short' and 'very short': and by colour: 'red', 'blue', 'green', 'yellow', etc. So, for example, if I need a moderately tall yellow one made of plastic I know precisely in which box to look.

Some of the tee-pegs bear the names of companies and golf courses on the stem, while others are blank. Although I don't know, because I haven't been able to find any information anywhere, my suspicion is that my most valuable ones will be those bearing a company name that for whatever reason is not around anymore. For example, I have a few with 'BCCI' on them, 'Thames TV Golf Society', 'Maxwell Communications', and my most prized one of all 'Fly Concorde', although the last named is a bit damaged.

How do I go about selling them through your auction? Would they be auctioned individually or by the box, or do you think they would fetch more as a collection?

Although I know it's difficult to say, do you have any idea what they might be worth?

Dear Head Greenkeeper at Royal Troon,

Like every other greenkeeper in the world, no doubt one of your biggest headaches is keeping your greens looking good and playing well. Members and visitors alike expect the greens to be smooth and true throughout the year and whatever the weather. Well, you will be thrilled to learn that your prayers have been answered and there's now a product that will both save you enormous amounts of money and provide the finest, truest greens in the world.

Although it looks and feels just like bentgrass, Omniturf has the enormous advantage in that it requires zero maintenance and is guaranteed to last for 25 years! Manufactured from a secret blend of some of the finest artificial fibres known to man, Omniturf behaves just like grass, looks just like grass and, thanks to our amazing boffins, even smells just like grass!

I'm sure you're now thinking this is just too good to be true. Well, what is even better is that we're willing to give – yes, GIVE – you a free demonstration. Here's the deal. Choose any one of your greens and, provided it's no bigger than 2500 square metres, we'll remove it and replace it with Omniturf to give you a chance to test if for yourself. The whole operation only takes a week.

We're extremely confident that after you've tried it, you'll want us to come back and do the lot. To give you some idea of cost, 18 average-sized greens generally works out at somewhere in the region of £1m. You'll probably save that in fertiliser, weedkiller and fungal treatments inside 24 months. And there's more money to be saved by firing most of the overpaid green staff and instead getting the comparatively cheap cleaners who look after the clubhouse to vacuum the greens about once a fortnight.

Dear Tee Distributor,

As distributors of golf equipment, you will appreciate the spectacular technological improvements that have been made in recent times. Titanium, graphite and other high tech materials have taken over from wood and steel.

Consequently, today's clubs and balls bear little resemblance to those our grandfathers used. Every facet of golf, including the bag, trolley and ball has undergone dramatic changes. Even the humble shoe spike has recently been transformed.

However, there is one tiny area where there has been absolutely no change at all. The tee-peg is precisely the same humble piece of wood it has always been. But I believe its days are numbered as I have developed the next generation of tee-peg.

Called the 'Eternitee', it has a number of remarkable features that its predecessor lacks. Firstly, it is a precision piece of equipment that can set the ball at precisely the same height off the ground every time. Secondly, it has a memory that will adjust that height to whatever is appropriate for the club you're using.

Thirdly, since it sits <u>on</u> the ground rather than <u>in</u> it, it reduces club deceleration on impact. Finally, because of an audible signal it emits five seconds after the shot, and every five seconds thereafter, it simply can't be lost. Hence, 'Eternitee'.

It works like this. The telescopic stem is controlled by a small chip in the base. The cup is also the dial, which turns so the arrow points to the number of whichever club is being used. The peg is most extended for a driver and most retracted for a lob wedge.

One of the chief advantages it has over the present peg is that you only need one instead of a number at different heights. Also, being made of titanium and virtually indestructible, you don't have to carry more than one in your pocket so no more embarrassing moments trying to locate your ball-marker in amongst a jumble of pegs.

Also worth mentioning is the fact that the battery is automatically recharged by the action of being struck. So, although at £49.99 it might seem expensive, it will last for years and save money in the long run.

Finally, by slashing the number of broken pegs littering the tees, it will help keep courses tidy whilst saving the planet by reducing waste.

Dear Lewis Hamilton,

As you know better than most, speed is a wonderful thing. And what impresses me about F1, even more than roaring down the straight at 200mph or thereabouts, is the speed with which they change your tyres. Compare the six or seven seconds they do it in with the one-and-a-half hours my local garage took to switch over my spare with the nearside front left about a fortnight ago.

Anyway, I gather you play golf and probably agree with me that it provides a far greater adrenaline rush than driving a car ever can. Going round and round the same circuit over and over again must be so dull that staying awake has to be a problem, surely. Whenever I feel a bit drowsy behind the wheel I switch on Radio 5 Live, which helps. Do you have a radio in your Mercedes or does all the clever technology take up so much space there's no room on the dashboard for the knobs?

Back to golf. For busy people like you and me, what we least like about the game is the inordinate amount of time it takes to play a round. Part of the problem is, of course, slow play but I'm afraid there is not a lot we can do about that. However, there is one area which I believes offers enormous scope and that is the buggies. Why do they have to be so slow? Probably because they don't want you to know how slow they really are, there's no speedometer but I would be surprised if their top speed was more than about 10mph. If you could raise that to, say, 50mph, think how much time that would save.

Why don't you have a word with the technical team at Mercedes and persuade them to design a sort of F1 golf buggy. We could call it the 'Hurry-up Hamilton', flog it to golf clubs all over the world and become obscenely rich, if you're not that already.

Dear Ryder Cup Organiser,

Although the Ryder Cup is undoubtedly one of the outstanding sporting occasions ranking alongside such other top events as the University Boat Race, the Grand National and the Eurovision Song Contest, I think there is a very real worry that one day things might get out of hand. Although quite a while ago, the War on the Shore in 1991 and the Battle of Brookline in 1999 are dramatic examples of what can go wrong when testosterone levels rise dangerously.

It's no good just wringing our hands and sighing, we must do something about it. What I'm proposing is a number of minor modifications to the format that I believe will ensure the Ryder Cup's survival as a great, international, sporting occasion whilst eliminating some of the less desirable aspects of it.

The problem, as I see it, is the matchplay format with its inherent confrontational character. Put two or four red-blooded guys in a head-to-head encounter and, inevitably, aggression will ensue and things can turn ugly. Then the crowd gets involved and events can spiral out of control before you can shout 'fore'! I've seen it on WWE wrestling and I fear we may see it again at a future Ryder Cup unless something is done.

Here's what I suggest. On day one, instead of foursomes in the morning and fourballs in the afternoon, why not kick off with a long-driving competition? Unlike the existing arrangement where only some of the guys get to play on the first two days, all 24 could drive, say, half-a-dozen balls. Each would hit one ball in turn with the US and Europe going alternately. To make it easier for the spectators and TV, the two sides could hit differently coloured balls. Only one ball from each player to count with the longest scoring 24 points and the shortest just one point.

Although I've not yet worked out all the details, other contests could include putting on a crazy course, a Texas scramble and a nearest the pin competition. Instead of three days of cut-throat matchplay, there would be a long weekend of fun and games. Instead of harsh words and mutual recrimination, there would be happiness and laughter. And, at the end, the winners would lift the trophy and the losers would at least have had a good time and maybe won an umbrella or two.

Dear Augusta National,

You will recall the little Welshman who won the US Masters quite a while back, Ian Woosnam. Well, by extraordinary coincidence he designed one of the two courses at my club, Dale Hill Hotel and Golf Club in East Sussex, England. So, in a sense, our two clubs are already inextricably bound together. My hope is to further strengthen the bonds between us so that despite the fact that we are separated by a great ocean and little bits of land at either end, we may forge a partnership that will survive for centuries and, incidentally, strengthen my bid for captaincy.

If I may explain that last bit. For some time now, I have felt that I should be elected captain at Dale Hill but, because of what I'm sure is nothing other than racial prejudice – something I'm sure Augusta National would never tolerate – I have been passed over. So I need to pull off an amazing coup, or something similar, to convince members that I should be captain.

May I suggest the following reciprocal arrangements as the first tentative couple of steps towards establishing closer ties between our clubs.

1) The winner of the US Masters be exempted from qualifying in the usual way for our biggest tournament, the Greenshield Trophy (a scratch competition ordinarily restricted to those who have won either a medal or Stableford competition in the previous 12 months). To even things up, I think the Greenshield Trophy winner should then automatically qualify for the following year's US Masters.

2) Both sets of members be offered the courtesy of the other's course so that Augusta National members visiting this country can play Dale Hill for nothing, while our members, who might find themselves in Augusta, can play your course for free. I feel compelled to warn you, however, that you'll find our greens are pretty quick, especially in summer.

Dear Open Championship Venue Selection Committee,

The British Open is undoubtedly one of the biggest events in the golfing calendar. However, I think there is a real danger of it becoming a bit stale. What do I mean? For example, it always seems to be held on a seaside course. These are pleasant enough and, watching the waves crashing on the shore, I'm sure helps players relax.

But what worries me is that foreigners viewing it on television will think that Britain is no more than just a length of coastline. What about all the pretty inland courses? Why are they never chosen to host the event?

Take my own club Dale Hill Hotel and Golf Club, just south of Tunbridge Wells. Apart from the fact that they use builders' sand in the bunkers, what's wrong with it? It has what I believe they call 'the necessary infrastructure', including a sauna and well stocked pro-shop.

Although the A21 is a bit slow in places, there's a 50-bedroom hotel which, assuming they are prepared to double up, could accommodate most of the field. There's a modest swimming pool, two dining rooms and a large selection of beers.

The car park presently only holds about 200 vehicles but it could be extended if necessary around the back of the greenkeeper's shed. What's more, and this is where it has the edge over, say, Muirfield, it has two courses. Splitting the field would make life a lot easier for you and remove the need for ridiculously early tee-off times.

I've spoken informally to the general manager and he has no objections in principle, although he didn't like the sound of a tented village 'flattening the grass', so we may have to look at that one. And care would have to be taken regarding dates so as not to clash with one of Dale Hill's biggest events, the July Cup. However, with goodwill on both sides, I see no reason why these obstacles can't be overcome.

Bringing The Open to this part of East Sussex will not only provide the local economy with a much-needed boost, I believe it will also refresh what is in danger of becoming a rather tired tournament and give the pros an exciting new challenge. Is it too late for next year?

Dear Roland McDonald,

Rather than try and fight this vegan thing, I would urge you to embrace it as you would a wounded cauliflower. Although vegetables aren't anywhere near as tasty as lovely meat, undoubtedly there is scope for producing dishes which are borderline edible. Combining my love for the great game of golf with a passion for cooking, I believe I have come up with something that will both appeal to your many customers as well as encourage them to take up golf.

To answer your anticipated question as to why McDonald's should encourage its clientele to take up golf, I would urge you to look at the size of some of them and think how desperately they need the exercise. By subtly encouraging them to participate in a healthy sport, you can claim to be doing your bit to combat obesity whilst continuing to flog essentially unhealthy burgers.

Called the 'McBunker', for reasons that will become apparent in a moment or two, my imaginative creation is something that you might particularly care to promote at around the time of the Open Championship. Traditionally held around the middle of July, it is the undoubted highlight of the golfing calendar.

Okay, I sense you want to know the recipe. Well, between the two halves of your bog-standard bun, you first slap down a bed of boiled cabbage. This represents the grass on the fairways and greens. In a scooped-out bit in the middle, you plonk a large spoonful of scrambled eggs, which of course represents the sand in the bunker. As for the ball, a single egg of cod's roe would do. If anyone complains that cod's roe isn't very white, you should explain that golf balls aren't always white and the one in their McBunker is one of those that isn't.

Although I experimented with a number of various ingredients to represent the rake, including trying to bend soggy twiglets, in the end what I thought worked best was shoving a plastic T-shaped toothpick into the top of the bun that was both fun and, by holding the whole thing together, was functional as well.

And so there you have it – a comparatively healthy burger that promotes healthy exercise.

Dear Desert Island Discs,

What's happened to Roy Plumtree? I ask because I was listening to Desert Island Discs the other day for the first time in quite a while and there was some woman asking all the questions. I've nothing against women *per se*, you understand, but it just didn't sound right.

Anyway, my point is the programme is sounding rather tired, worse even than me after 18 holes of golf. The problem, as I see it, is there are far too many what you might call celebrities and far too few ordinary people. Look back over the last 50 years or thereabouts and you could hardly claim your guest list is composed of a representative sample of humanity. Showbiz grotesquely outnumbers every other area of human endeavour while my extensive research has failed to reveal even one golfer. Mind you, I can't blame you for not inviting Sir Nick Faldo onto your show because he is irredeemably dull.

The problem with celebrities is they are rather inclined to bang on about their glitzy lifestyle leaving us Radio 4 listeners feeling like failures just because we never starred in a movie, had a number one hit, wrote a best-selling novel or won a Nobel Prize.

The other thing about them is they choose music they think will impress listeners. We don't want dreary classical rubbish. Most people like music you can dance to or singalong with.

Assuming you're persuaded by the strength of my argument that you need more ordinary people to be marooned on your desert island where, you might wonder, will you find a decent cross-section of the nicer elements in our society? The answer might surprise you. Having spent a fair bit of my life in there, I can tell you that you need look no further than the spike bar at my local golf club. There are all sorts in there… scratch golfers, high handicappers, single figure players, the lot. There are even women!

To kick things off, you might care to invite me as I've a fund of riveting anecdotes and golf stories that I'm confident will amuse your listeners. That and some great music from the likes of Freddie and the Dreamers, the Monkees, the Yardbirds and Billy Fury should make for a brilliant show. How about it, BBC?

Dear Institute for Dream Studies,

Because it might contribute to your understanding of golfers, their frustrations and often fragile mental state, I should like to share with you a recurring dream I have had every night for the past 40 years. In it I'm standing on the 18th green at St Andrews delivering the following speech:

'Your Royal Highness, members of the R&A, fellow golfers everywhere. Believe me, I'm as surprised as you are that I'm the Open Champion and holding this beautiful trophy. As my previous best performance was 38 points in a mid-week

Stableford competition, this win has to go down as the biggest of my career.

Looking at the list of former champions engraved here – Henry Cotton, Bobby Jones, Arnold Palmer, Jack Nicklaus and, who's this, Ben Curtis? – fills me with humility. Incidentally, Merriweather is spelt with an 'i' not a 'y'. (Turning to one side and in a low voice) Can they fix that before I take it home?

I would first of all like to commiserate with Bryson DeChambeau, who must have thought his four-shot lead going into today's final round would be sufficient. We had a great battle out there and I was just fortunate that my 40-foot, triple-breaking, birdie putt on the final extra hole found the back of the cup while his seemingly straightforward two-footer surprisingly lipped out.

I would also like to mention Jeremy Foskett, who said I would never play decent golf with a strong grip. (Waving trophy) Look at me now, Jeremy! To Nigel 'Duck Hook' Armitage, who left me out of the Dale Hill team for the vital veterans' fixture against Sedlescombe last week because he didn't think I could handle the pressure. (Waving trophy) Look at me now, Nigel!

To all my various playing partners who, over the years, have offered a wide variety of useless tips, I should like to say 'thank you' for your kind, if somewhat misguided, advice.

Finally, let me make it clear that I shall not be turning professional or participating in any future European or USPGA tour events. Nor do I wish to be considered for the European Ryder Cup team (loud groans of disappointment).

Today I've achieved all that I have ever wanted and I shall now withdraw gracefully from competitive golf to concentrate on writing my book and getting my handicap down to where it should be, which is about 17. Thank you.'

Dear Met Office,

Have you ever heard of Bryson DeChambeau? Don't worry if you haven't as I suspect he won't have heard of Michael Fish, Carol Kirkwood or Tomasz Schafernaker. Anyway, although he's rather slow when playing golf and, frankly, a bit of a 'nutter', he's nevertheless a very successful American golfer who's won quite a few important tournaments.

Rather like a lot of the boffins that I suspect work at the Met Office, he's something of a mad scientist. Anyway, he approaches golf in much the same way as you do the weather. For example, I don't suppose that you hang bits of seaweed outside your office or believe it's going to rain just because the cows are sitting down. Well, DeChambeau analyses all the data before taking a shot, which is one of the reasons he plays so slowly.

Although he's a bit creepy, you can't argue with his performances. Anyway, one of the vital variables he takes into account is air density and I'm wondering if there might be any commercial benefit to you in producing Air Density Forecasts. You needn't bother with the whole country, just places like St Andrews, Sunningdale, The Belfry, Sandwich, Muirfield, etc.

I don't want to be paid for the idea, all I ask is that I be allowed to audition for the job of presenting the daily Air Density Forecasts on TV.

Dear António Guterres,

What with wars, famine and disease, not to mention global pandemics, I appreciate that you've got your work cut out and I therefore hesitate to involve you in something which might at first glance appear to be quite trivial. However, because of the international nature of the problem I honestly believe that you are in an ideal position to sort it out.

Although I respect that different countries have different traditions and different ways of doing things, there are times when uniformity would be to everyone's benefit. Take plug sockets for example. If every country could agree to have the same number and shape pins, travelling would be much easier and you could take your hairdryer all over the world.

Since I'm an old man with very little hair, I'm less concerned about hair dryers than I am about golf. The specific problem that I've encountered on the golf courses of the world that you might be able to fix concerns the markers that indicate how far you are from the green.

Firstly, there are all sorts of different colours. Secondly, the markers are of varying distances from the green. Thirdly, they can be in either yards or metres. And, finally, sometimes they indicate the distance to the front of the green and sometimes to the centre.

As a result, the poor visiting golfer is utterly confused. (As indeed might you be if you're not a golfer and can't altogether appreciate the problem I'm trying to describe.) Although you might presume that this is something that the various governing bodies of golf should sort out, I fear that, because of petty rivalries and jealousies, they won't. It therefore needs a respected global figure of great stature to intervene.

Initially, however, it might help if someone were to visit the principal golfing nations of the world. play on the main championship courses and report back to you. Now that I am more or less retired, I have the time and would be happy to take on this awesome task as an official UN Ambassador.

Perhaps after you've raised the issue in the General Assembly and/or Security Council, you could let me know how much I'm going to earn and what sort of bar expenses would be considered acceptable.

Dear Rolex,

Although I know it sounds ridiculous, nothing in this world is more important to me than punctuality. Take this letter for example. The letterbox at the end of my road is emptied daily (except Sundays) at 4.45pm and so there I will be at 4.44pm this afternoon dropping it in. Because they care less about punctuality than I do, the Royal Mail often don't empty the box until after 5pm; I know because I can see it from my bedroom window.

Not only am I a remarkably punctual person, I am also a keen golfer. The two are not entirely unrelated as timing is a key component of the golf swing and turning up on the tee on time is absolutely vital, which brings me seamlessly onto the need to replace my present timepiece.

Unfortunately, the black silicone strap broke on my present watch at the top of my backswing hurling the important bit straight into the ball-washer thereby dislocating one of Mickey's arms. Sod's law dictated it was the right arm which, since you're in the business, you probably already know indicates the hour and so I now can tell it's, say, 20 minutes past something but 20 minutes past what? Consequently, I can be an hour early or, much worse, an hour late, which is absolutely hopeless.

From reading your advertisements, I gather that you have struck deals with a number of top players. My suspicion is you probably give them a decent wedge (not lofted ☺) as well as one of your watches. Well, if you were to enrol me as a Rolex ambassador, you would only have to supply a watch as I wouldn't demand any money. Not only would I wear your watch with pride but I believe ordinary handicap golfers would also more easily identify with me than they do with a bunch of self-satisfied, super-rich, smug bastards who just so happen to be exceptionally good at golf.

Dear Archers' Producer,

I must confess that I don't listen to the Archers very often. However, on those infrequent occasions when I do, I quite enjoy it.

Having said that, I feel that the time has come to shift the social focus away from The Bull. Apart from anything else, I feel that it might, in some subliminal way, encourage drinking. Although I don't think it should be demolished to make way for an Ambridge bypass or be destroyed by a meteor, I do think that another regular venue should be found that has a more healthy and wholesome appeal.

Having given it a great deal of thought, I believe I have come up with the perfect solution. Since agriculture is almost certainly in terminal decline in this country, alternative uses must be found for farmland. And what better use could there possibly be than recreational?

So I suggest you convert a chunk of Home Farm (about 250 acres should be sufficient) into 'Ambridge Golf and Country Club'.

Golf is a great game and offers enormous opportunities for characters to interact. Then there are the competitions. Provided we can find a way to persuade the bulk of Ambridge inhabitants to quickly reach an acceptable standard of play, you could have sworn enemies meeting in the final of, say, the Walter Gabriel Memorial Trophy.

Mixed foursomes matches, traditionally rather fraught affairs, offer scope for all sorts of intrigue and naughtiness. If you decide to take up my idea, then by way of thanks, would you kindly audition me for the part of the club professional? Incidentally, if he's still alive, I think Jack Woolley would make an ideal club captain.

Dear Pfizer,

Before I go any further, would you kindly settle an argument that broke out in the spike bar of my golf club recently between myself and Harvey 'Three Putts' Harrison as to whether or not you pronounce the 'P' in Pfizer. My argument was that you do pronounce the 'P' otherwise why would it be there?

Before I go further still, may I congratulate you wholeheartedly on discovering a vaccine for that appalling Coronavirus thing that not only has killed dozens of people all over the world but caused the postponement of the US Masters, the cancellation of The Open and basically ruined my summer. I'm just hoping that I'm not among the unfortunate 10 per cent or thereabouts for whom your remedy apparently doesn't work.

Having dealt the pandemic a mortal blow, doubtless you are looking around wondering what to do next. After all, you can't afford to have all those white-coated boffins sitting around in your well-equipped laboratories twiddling their thumbs while waiting for the next nasty bug to escape from one of those disgusting Chinese markets where they sell all manner of diseased wild animals, can you? In retrospect, I think my mother was absolutely right in refusing to ever eat in a Chinese restaurant. 'You never know what's lurking beneath those huge piles of rice,' she used to say.

Back to business. For some years now I have suffered from an affliction that blights the career of many a golfer for which, as yet, there is no known cure. Called the 'yips', its name suggests it might also have originated in China. Without going into too much detail, it's a sort of involuntary muscle spasm that renders putting an absolute nightmare. Golfers suffering from it would, I'm certain, pay vast sums to be cured.

If you would approach the problem with the same commitment, enthusiasm and determination you so admirably displayed when battling Coronavirus, I'm confident you could have a pill, vaccine or whatever available in all good pro shops before very long.

Finally, with regard to enrolling volunteers, I would happily put myself forward on condition you promise not to fob me off with some worthless placebo.

○○○○○

Dear Eton College Headmaster,

I'm writing to enquire as to whether you would consider offering golf to your pupils as an alternative to the Wall Game. From the little I've seen of the latter, it seems decidedly rough and dangerous.

Not only is golf safe and civilised by comparison, it is also absolutely ideal for young toffs looking to make their way in the world of banking, stock broking, insider trading, money laundering and the like.

If you are prepared to consider it, I should like to offer my services as head golf coach. A 19 handicapper with an elegant shoulder turn but a rather strong grip, I honestly believe I could have won a couple of majors if only I had taken up the game earlier, instead of wasting my time playing football. At the dodgy school I went to there was no choice. Now I'm keen to give others the chance that I never had.

Eton is fortunate in having plenty of playing fields, one of which could be used as a sort of driving range. And then I would hope there is a possibility that we could borrow the nine-hole course I understand the infamous Prince Andrew has laid out in a corner of Windsor Great Park.

No doubt you're quite chummy with the Royals and so a request from you will stand a much better chance of succeeding than one coming from me.

Dear European Tour,

In a world of finite resources where we all have a duty to conserve energy and reduce waste, how can professional golfers justify teeing up a brand new golf ball every couple of holes? Surely this is just profligate nonsense that flies in the face, not so much of bunkers, but of responsible behaviour. From my own considerable experience as a 19-handicapper, I can say with some authority that new balls behave no better and fly no further than averagely scuffed balls. So why do pros frequently discard a perfectly decent ball to tee up a new one? One obvious explanation is that they are given an endless supply of them for which they don't have to pay and so there's no incentive for them to be less wasteful.

Furthermore, the manufacture of golf balls clearly contributes to golf's carbon footprint and thus to climate change. Although my club (Dale Hill Hotel and Golf Club) is thankfully nearly 300 feet above sea level, the same is not true of the dozens of magnificent links courses stretched around our glorious coastline. Muirfield, Turnberry, Royal St George's, Rye, Royal Portrush, Trevose, Troon and dozens of others are extremely vulnerable to even a modest rise in sea level. Do we really want the Old Course at St Andrews to only be playable at low tide? Will we be happy that greenkeepers will not only rake the bunkers but drag seaweed off the greens as well? Of course not! And so this is why the European Tour must introduce a

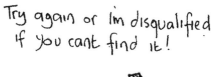

rule that requires pros to only use one ball per round. If they lose it, they are out of the tournament.

Although this may sound harsh, in my opinion it will have the very beneficial effect of discouraging players from hitting the ball too far. For some time now the authorities have been worried about courses being overwhelmed by the 'bombers' but have been frightened to act for fear of being sued by the equipment manufacturers. Well, this could be the answer!

In recognition of helping to save both the planet and the game of golf, all I ask is that the new rule that requires players to only use one ball be called 'Mortimer's Rule'. In that way, although I've never won a major, my name will be immortalised as long as the game of golf is played.

Dear Guinness,

When people think of Ireland, which three things immediately spring to mind? Well, I believe they are Guinness, golf and dodgy priests doing unmentionable things to young children. Discarding the last one for reasons of good taste, let's focus on the other two – your magnificent beer and the greatest game on earth.

A creative thinker who makes a modest living by coming up with wholly original ideas to sell to large companies such as yours, I have what I believe is a genius idea that I'm confident will boost consumption of Guinness wherever the game of golf is played.

Called the 'Guinness Golfball Giveaway', it's remarkably simple really and works like this. Whenever a customer orders a pint of Guinness, the barman or barwoman asks them, 'Do you want to tee-off?' If the customer says 'yes', the barman or barwoman proceeds to ask them a question about the Irish Open Golf Championship, such as, 'Who won it in 1927?' If they answer, 'George Duncan' and provided they buy another pint of Guinness, they go through to the next round.

In round two they have to answer a simple question on the rules of golf. For example, 'If the player lifts his or her ball at rest or causes it to move, the ball must be replaced on its original spot (which if not known must be estimated) (see Rule 14.2), except in two specific circumstances: can you give me either of them? The correct answer is either when the player lifts the ball under a Rule to take relief or to replace the ball on a different spot (see Rules 14.2d and 14.2e), or when the ball moves only after the player has begun the stroke or the backswing for a stroke and then goes on to make the stroke. It's entirely at the discretion of the barman or barwoman to decide whether the customer's answer is correct. If it is and provided they buy another pint, they can proceed to the third and final question on famous Irish golfers. Here the questions inevitably are a tad harder such as: how old was Christy O'Connor Snr when he died in 2016? The correct answer, of course, is 91. Everyone who gets three correct answers in a row wins a golf ball.

One of the great attractions of the 'Guinness Golfball Giveaway' is that it can easily be adapted to any country simply by tailoring the questions to that country. For example in Kazakhstan, question one would be about the Kazakhstan

Open; question two would be about the rules of golf and question three would be about famous Kazakhstan golfers.

I'm happy to research and script all the questions for which I would ask a modest 10,000 Euros per country.

Dear Footjoy,

The traffic is horrific and it looks like you're going to be late on the first tee and incur a two-shot penalty. You pull up in the car park but you've not yet changed your shoes. Don't panic because you're wearing a pair of Kwikswitcher shoes. Just leap out of the car and clip a pair of spiked soles onto them – soft or hard spikes depending on the conditions. And then crunch an imperious drive down the first.

On the tricky par three, you hit your tee-shot a bit fat and just fail to carry the stream that guards the green. Your ball is lying in shallow water and is distinctly playable but you don't want to play the rest of the round with wet feet. Nor do you want to take a penalty drop. Fortunately, you've remembered the 'growtall' attachment is in your bag and so you simply unclip your spiked soles and snap on the six-inch platform soles. After you've splashed out, you stick your spikes back on and hole the putt for par. Incidentally, I tried installing the platforms inside the shoes so that they would automatically inflate when they made contact with water, in much the same way as do lifeboats in aircraft, but I experienced too many mishaps when simply striding down slightly soggy fairways.

Back to our story. You win the match and, as you walk off the 18th green, your dejected opponent shakes your hand and then disappears into the locker-room to change his shoes whereas all you have to do is unclip your spikes and, hey presto, you're now back into town shoes and ready for that celebratory pint.

You will be aware of how expensive shoes are these days, especially decent golf shoes. What shall we say, £100? So three pairs will cost £300. Instead, a pair of Kwikswitchers will only set you back a modest £125, thus saving you £175! And you can save a whole lot more when you buy any of the numerous accessories including snap-on ice-blades, crampons, football boots, ballet shoes and roller-blades.

Since my knowledge of the boot and shoe industry is somewhat limited, I'm wondering if you would like to buy my patented design and take over the entire project. Does £250,000 all-in sound reasonable?

Dear Andy Murray,

First of all, belated congratulations on winning so many tennis matches during your extremely illustrious career. Mrs Merriweather (my late mother) was a huge fan of yours and, frankly, news of your first bungled hip operation almost certainly contributed to her untimely death aged 101. But as I, too, have a dodgy hip, I can probably empathise with your plight more than she did. Incidentally, may I politely enquire how you were able to have your recent operation organised so quickly when I've been waiting ages for mine? Perhaps the NHS queue north of the border is shorter than it is in Sussex. Well, I suppose it's only fair there are compensations for living in such a bleak place with such awful weather, stodgy food and having to listen to dreary bagpipes.

Anyway, when you've had enough of your comeback and you're considering what you're going to do in the future, may I make a suggestion? Although you will doubtless be tempted to take up commentating or coaching, I would urge you to continue competing, but at golf not tennis. Golf is so much better than tennis; it's much friendlier – apart from the occasional 'fore!' no one yells – and it's a lot less tiring.

I read somewhere that, although brother Jamie was better at golf, you were a half-decent single-figure player in your youth until you foolishly switched to tennis. With a few lessons, I'm sure you would soon be playing well enough to compete on the European Tour. Remember, golfers traditionally don't peak until their late-30s and so time is on your side. To the best of my knowledge, no one has ever won a tennis grand slam AND a golf major. By becoming the first, you would secure your place in the pantheon of great British sportsmen and, because I know you're a bit funny about it, sportswomen.

As you are already fairly well-known, I'm absolutely certain that, if you did become a pro golfer, you would receive dozens of sponsors' invites to play in the very best, most lucrative tournaments. You would only need to make a few cuts and secure the odd top-ten finish to earn enough to retain your card and stay on the tour.

To help keep the cost down, I'd be willing to carry your bag for free – for the first couple of years at least. 'Mortimer and Murray' has a ring to it, don't you think?

Come on, Andy – let's do it!

Dear Michael O'Leary,

'Mr O'Leary is a commercial genius,' I told my friend Arnold recently when we were flying Ryanair from Shannon to Gatwick after a lovely golfing holiday in County Clare. To be precise, because we were sitting 15 rows apart as a result of your inspired policy of separating travel companions unless they're prepared to stump up the extra, I said it to him as we were walking into the south terminal at Gatwick.

Of all your innovations, I think extorting a penal charge from suckers who, for whatever reason, don't have a boarding pass is perhaps your single greatest contribution to modern travel. Anyway, I have a suggestion which, if implemented, should provide a fitting boost to what appears to be your sagging bottom line.

Not that it matters to you one grimy Euro how rich or poor are the customers you fleece but there is, perhaps, a tad more satisfaction in ripping off the rich. Anyway, golfers generally are fairly well off and so could be regarded as legitimate targets. Although you already extort a fortune for carrying clubs in the hold, there is undoubted scope for squeezing a bit more from the unwary hackers. Since no golfer has a clue as to what the circumference of his bag is, you could apply a maximum limit of, say, 25inches which, although sounding generous, would catch out all but the smallest bags. Trust me, very few would slip through the net. Alternatively, you could stipulate a maximum of 13 clubs which, since nearly every golfer has a full-set of 14, should generate substantial extra revenue. Or why not do both and enjoy a double bonanza?

Doubtless you have a 'Fleecing Unit' which could assess my suggestions and I hardly need advise you, or them, of the need to slip something in very small type somewhere near the bottom of the terms and conditions. Renowned for respecting the rules, golfers should take the penalty on the chin.

Dear DJ Spoony,

As a black man yourself, you will be aware of the awful prejudice that exists in many sectors of our society. And, as a golfer, you know that, to its enormous shame, the game which we both love has hardly blazed a progressive trail. As a regular golfer, I'm frequently shocked both by the appalling prejudices manifested by my playing partners and, even more insulting, the casual assumption they make that I must share their ugly opinions. To my considerable shame, rather than disabuse them, I simply say nothing and hope that they might cotton on to the fact that I don't agree with them.

What I've been searching for is a discreet but effective way of indicating to those with whom I play golf that I'm not bigoted and the solution came to me on the short 15th at Dale Hill Hotel and Golf Club … a black ball. Because it symbolises rejection, a black ball would, in my opinion, be a particularly appropriate method of conveying the message, 'Shut up, bigot!'

What I'm suggesting, therefore, is that an approach be made to one of the major golf ball manufacturers urging them to produce a ball and make a modest donation to Black Lives Matter for every one sold. After fairly extensive field tests with a few that I painted myself, I found them perfectly satisfactory in every respect other than they are fiendishly difficult to follow in flight and then to find. Still, I'm confident 'we will overcome' this slight obstacle.

Your support in this venture would be greatly appreciated.

Dear Office Furniture Manufacturer,

You will be aware, I'm sure, of the strong liking our captains of industry and business leaders have for the game of golf. Even the very briefest of glances through *Who's Who* and the hobbies of the rich and famous reveals an astonishing fondness for it.

Furthermore, I believe that this fact can be commercially exploited by a combination of my considerable knowledge of the game and your considerable knowledge of the fascinating world of office furniture.

I therefore propose that we jointly examine the feasibility of reproducing some of the most famous greens in the world in the offices of some of the most powerful men and women on the planet.

If you've ever watched golf on television, you will have seen the computer-generated graphics that are often used to illustrate the slope on a green. The information that we need, therefore, is already available and I don't suppose it would be much of a problem to persuade the relevant TV companies to release it to us.

All we would need to do is convert this information into three dimensional carpets, with some form of foam supporting the raised areas. The foam would need to be fairly resilient in order to create an authentic turf-like feel and care would need to be taken to ensure that the texture of the surface material, the carpet if you like, possesses similar qualities to a close-cut lawn so that putting on it would be just like putting on the green itself. We could even check the speed of the carpets with the same device used by tournament officials, a stimpmeter.

The only problem I can foresee is making adjustments to the rest of the office furniture to allow for the slope. For example, three of the legs on the desk might need to be shortened to ensure that the top was horizontal. Because this furniture might get moved around, rather than simply saw off legs at the bottom, it would perhaps be desirable to make the legs adjustable.

And I would suggest the hole itself be movable to even out the wear and tear and to provide the occupant with a variety of challenging putts. I suggest we start with a range of 18th greens taken from such great courses as St Andrews, Wentworth, Carnoustie, Pebble Beach and Augusta. These could be split into ranges. How about the British Open, Ryder Cup, and US Open with six in each?

Clearly, with offices being predominantly rectangular and of different sizes, we would simply take a rectangular chunk out of each green. Bunkers in the form of sunken sofas could be an optional extra.

Dear Sky Sports,

Until Sky appeared there was very little golf on TV and so I say 'well done' for bringing us so much great golf from around the world.

My purpose in writing is to make a suggestion that I think will improve your coverage considerably. Unlike football, where Sky has come up with a number of exciting innovations, the golf coverage has remained pretty much the same. One camera on the tee, another behind the green and occasionally one on the fairway with a sound man picking up the tedious discussion between player and caddie as to which way the wind is blowing.

Why not insert cameras into the heads of the putters of the main contenders? Then, as the player lines up to stroke the ball, we at home will get a unique view of the putt. Admittedly, things might go a little awry as the player follows through after the putt but staying with it might provide some unusual shots of cloud formations and so on. You're not called Sky for nothing!

To anticipate a rather obvious concern that players won't welcome bulky cameras and attendant wires hanging off their putters, you know as well as I do that cameras these days are very small so that even the most sensitive players will hardly notice them.

If, as I expect, this proves enormously popular, you could extend the experiment to include other clubs such as drivers and the like. And another place cameras could be sited is in the flagsticks. A recent rule amendment allows players to leave the flag in when they putt. Perhaps you could lobby to make leaving the flag in compulsory and train the caddies to turn the stick so that the lens is facing whoever is putting. Caddies generally are accommodating chaps and would, I'm sure, be happy to cooperate, especially if you bung them a few beers after the round.

Ultimately, of course, a camera inside the ball offers the unbelievably exciting prospect of a totally fresh perspective on the game. But that, like the players' unbelievable drives, might be way off in the distance.

Dear Dalai Lama,

As I understand it, you are the spiritual leader of all the Buddhists in the world. Although they're relatively thin on the ground as compared with the more common Christians and Muslims, there are, I've discovered, over 500 million of your lot. Why then do I not meet more Buddhists? I know a lot of Christians, a surprising number of Jews, a sprinkling of Muslims and quite a few atheists but I can't claim to know even one, actual, practising Buddhist. They're certainly not down the Dog and Duck on a Friday night and so, where are they all? They make up seven per cent of the world's population and so, statistically speaking, one in 14 of the people I bump into shopping in Sainsbury's should be Buddhists; and even more in the organic fruit and vegetable section. Because they don't all wear the gear you do, I suppose it's possible there are more around than I realise.

Let me move swiftly on to *my* religion... golf. I don't suppose either the topography or the climate is suitable up there in Tibet for the Royal and Ancient game but, from what I know of Buddhism, it strikes me as the ideal game for your followers. It's very Zen, you see. And being outside in the fresh air with glorious scenery and so close to nature, it stimulates all sorts of profound communing with the natural forces that govern everything. Not only that but golf also has its mantras such as, 'Keep your head down', 'Left arm straight', 'Swing smoothly' and 'Don't miss for God's sake.' And a belief in reincarnation brings hope to those of us who dream of coming back as a scratch golfer.

So what I'm proposing is running a series of retreats at Dale Hill Hotel and Golf Club near Ticehurst in East Sussex exclusively for Buddhists wishing to both come to a greater understanding of life whilst at the same time lowering their handicaps. Called 'Birdies for Buddhists' it would be a week-long retreat. Each day would begin with a quiet period of calm and reflection followed by a short-game clinic, a veggie burger and chips for lunch, a round of golf in the afternoon, a peaceful session in the spike bar before a bit of chanting and an early night.

It would certainly help me sell the package if you would be willing to endorse it. Something like, *'Improve both your golf and your chances of a better life next time around with Birdies for Buddhists – D Lama.'*

Dear JP McManus,

Although a couple might have dropped dead since the article was written, I read somewhere that you presently own 550 racehorses. It might be a fun idea to organise an enormous race for all your horses to find out which is the best. Imagine 550 horses thundering down an especially widened track. Wouldn't that be an amazing spectacle? Apart from finding a wide enough racecourse, one problem might be getting hold of 550 sets of your distinctive green and gold silks. And I don't envy the racecourse commentator identifying all the runners and riders. Anyway, I'm contacting you as one golfer to another in the hope that you might be able to help me.

Presumably thinking up names for all your horses must be quite a headache. Well, I have a ready-made name that I would be absolutely thrilled for you to use. To be completely straight with you, the idea behind it is to send a very clear message to the committee at my golf club, Dale Hill, that there is one man who has been repeatedly overlooked for the captaincy and that man is me! And so the name that I would be delighted for you to use is Captain Merriweather, which I think sounds rather good, don't you?

Assuming you like the name as much as I do, may I ask that you save it for one of your better nags? Although it might sound a little unreasonable, how disappointing it would be for me if it ended up running in low grade races at, say, Newton Abbot or Bangor-on-Dee. And how much more impact it would have on the committee if it, say, won the Grand National or the Cheltenham Gold Cup. If it did win a big race, I would happily grab the horse's head on one side while you took the other so that we could jointly lead it into the winner's enclosure.

Although I recognise my idea is a 25/1 shot, stranger things have happened in racing. Remember Foinavon? Which wasn't one of yours, I don't think.

○○○○○

Dear Mr Djokovic,

Although I'm not a world number one, or ever likely to be, I believe I understand what I think is your problem. It's certainly not your backhand, which is pretty solid, but rather it is your astonishing lack of popularity. You would think, wouldn't you, that the greatest tennis player in the world would be hugely popular. But you're obviously not, which evidently upsets you because, like most of us, you want to be loved.

I've not conducted a formal survey but, supplied with three alternative answers to the question, 'Which of the following most accurately describes Novak Djokovic?' my hunch is that here in the UK (obviously in Serbia things are somewhat different) the answers would roughly be as follows:

A) A brilliant tennis player and a worthy champion whom I much admire 5%

B) An arrogant and ill-tempered tosser who behaves like a spoilt child 30%

C) A complete cock 65%

What I suspect you want to know is: how do you go about improving your image and popularity rating? Well, let me tell you about a bloke at my golf club, Dale Hill. Let's call him Roger. A scratch golfer who has won the club championship no fewer than 20 times and nearly all the other club competitions for which he is eligible, he is always magnanimous in victory and gracious on those rare occasions he loses. He never sulks nor has ever thrown a club in his life. Considering how good he is, he is remarkably modest and friendly to everyone, even the very high handicappers! I sincerely believe you should try and be more like Roger.

There is one more thing I would like to suggest and that is to cut out that ridiculous nonsense when you win a final and point to the ceiling and then throw your arms out to the four corners of the arena. What the f*** is that all about? It looks like you're reaching up to God and acting as a conduit to draw down his love to then share with the spectators. It might be as well to remember that you're just a professional tennis player and not the frigging messiah!

Dear LGBT Foundation,

I would very much welcome your advice as to how I should go about changing my gender from male to female. Is it just a case of me simply self-identifying as a woman? If that's all it is and there's no requirement to undergo any unpleasant surgery, I'm up for it.

To be honest, it's not a question of always having felt myself to be a woman, as I never have. In case you're curious to know why an octogenarian gentleman and lifelong misogynist should want to switch sides, so to speak, I shall explain.

I'm a very keen, if not terribly accomplished, golfer. As I get older, I'm increasingly finding the par fours are not, as they're supposed to be, reachable in two. Anything over 350 yards is frankly way out of my range. Sure, I could get on in three and then hole the putt for par but my putting is pretty awful and so I very rarely single putt.

I have therefore come to the conclusion that the only way I could reach most of the par fours in regulation is to shorten the holes by playing off the forward red tees. However these, as I'm sure you are aware, are reserved for women. Ah, now do you understand my situation?

Another worthwhile benefit I would enjoy if I switched over is a significantly reduced membership subscription at my club, Dale Hill. For some arcane reason, women pay less.

Finally, the women's section is very much smaller than the men's and so the odds of me being elected Women's Captain would be significantly shorter than they are of being elected Men's Captain which, frankly, seems increasingly unlikely.

And having stumbled into the women's locker room one evening after a particularly boozy session with the boys, I appreciate how much more fragrant and appealing it is compared to the men's.

Dear President Bolsonaro,

I've always wanted to visit Brazil (why some people spell it with an 's' baffles me). Any country that produces outstanding footballers such as Pele must be doing something right, eh? More than anything else, I would love to explore the Amazon Basin which, thanks to your enlightened 'slash and burn' policy, must be far more accessible now.

I appreciate that the primary purpose of burning so many millions of hectares was to provide your farmer friends with cheap land but now that so much impenetrable jungle has been eliminated, there exists a unique opportunity to build hundreds of decent hotels and top-notch visitor attractions. And there should be more than enough space left over to create dozens, if not hundreds, of first-class golf courses. Providing them will help Brazil attract more of the right sort of tourist and fewer Sir David Attenboroughs, if you know what I mean.

As things stand, apart from the carnival in Rio and the odd sandy beach, Brazil hasn't a great deal to offer today's discerning traveller. Furthermore, golf courses would provide suitable employment – caddies, greenkeepers, bar staff and the like – for those who have inadvertently been displaced. By introducing them to the joy of golf, it might even stop them dwelling on the destruction of their former way of life. As a further sop, you might care to use your considerable influence to persuade the courses to offer genuine indigenous folk a 15% discount on the regular green fees.

From a political perspective, by helping to establish your country as an appealing destination that offers exceptional golf in a unique jungle-like setting, you will create a legacy as a visionary leader rather than the arsehole in exile facing multiple charges back home.

Dear DP World Tour,

Why is golf's popularity waning? Is it because it's virtually impossible for ordinary people to hit the ball straight or is it because golf clubs are horribly stuffy places that positively discourage visitors? Well, after giving the matter considerable thought I believe that I at least have an explanation as to why the viewing figures for DP World Tour events on TV are dropping while, if you'll forgive the joke, my putts aren't?

The explanation in a word is 'technology'. While other sports featured on TV have embraced it, golf hasn't. Take tennis for example. The loathsome Djokovic hits a backhand that appears to land very close to the base line. Is it in or out? The tension mounts as Hawk-Eye follows the ball's trajectory and … it's out! Yippee!

Moving onto cricket and England are once again struggling with only the likeable Joe Root seemingly capable of stopping the horrible Aussies from bowling us out for a miserably low score. And then he's hit on the pad. The horrible Aussies all leap in the air and appeal. Oh no, the umpire has raised his finger and the horrible Aussies are ecstatic. Root thinks for a moment and then gives the 'T' sign indicating he wants the decision reviewed. The whole of England holds its breath as DRS (Decision Review System) swings into action. Bad news as a combination of 'Snicko' and 'Hot Spot' reveal the ball didn't touch the bat. Will Hawk-Eye save Rooty? One red light, two red lights but the third red light fails to illuminate as the predicted path of the ball is just clearing the off bail. Joe's not out and the horrible Aussies are gutted. Yippee!

Although not universally popular, the Video Assistant Referee (VAR) has certainly added another dimension to watching football on TV. It increases the tension and contributes considerable controversy whilst relieving the linesmen (no-one calls them assistant referees) of the awesome responsibility of deciding whether or not a goal-scorer was offside.

Sadly, golf has nothing to compete with the above and so I suggest you adapt VAR to determine whether or not a player was in front of the marker when teeing off. For example, the extremely unlikeable Bryson DeChambeau hits what appears to be a magnificent tee-shot on a par three that finishes just a few inches from the hole. His unattractive face lights up. But hang on, was his left foot a fraction in front of where it should have been? Yes, VAR indicates it was and it's a two-shot penalty. DeChambeau goes purple with rage. Yippee! How entertaining is that?

Dear Mike Ashley,

I know you're a big football fan but have no idea if you play golf. It's an expensive game but great fun. Provided the committee is not composed entirely of Newcastle United supporters who despise you for screwing their club for fourteen barren seasons, you should have no difficulty joining somewhere. Having said that, some of the smarter clubs might frown a bit on your background in retail and your rather rough demeanour. But, as I'm sure you're aware, money talks and so you might be admitted at a club which, ten years ago, would have regarded you as totally unacceptable.

Anyway, my purpose in writing is to alert you to a great business opportunity connected with golf. Those who love the game are suckers for anything connected with it, particularly the famous courses where punters will pay ludicrous sums for monogrammed sweaters and golf balls.

Why should golf clubs nick all this valuable business? What I'm suggesting we do is make available to the public through your Sports Direct stores, a range of products that are both unusual and yet have historic associations. For example, an egg timer filled with sand from one of the world's most famous bunkers, such as the one guarding the 17th green at St Andrews. By the way, that's a course in Scotland, not Birmingham City's home ground. Then there could be bottles of perfume based on water extracted from such famous hazards as the Swilken Burn at St Andrews and Rae's Creek at Augusta National in the USA. Aftershave, too, could be distilled from mowings shaven from the fairways of Carnoustie in Scotland and Pebble Beach in the States. The possibilities are endless.

The real genius is that these products only need contain some sand, water or whatever from these famous places. One grain per million or one drop per 1000 gallons would be sufficient to enable us to legitimately claim they contain the genuine article. Each packet would include a certificate of authenticity signed by a respected individual widely acknowledged as someone of proven stature, honesty and integrity... you?

I can see the egg timers being knocked out for something like £29.99, the aftershave for £69.99 and the perfume for £99.99. Are you in?

Dear Black Lives Matter,

Can anyone tell me why professional golfers don't 'take a knee' by kneeling down while hitting their opening tee-shot in tournaments? Not only would that make a bold statement about how much black lives matter but it would also reveal who are the genuinely gifted ball strikers.

You might be interested to learn that I was going to suggest that all competitors 'take a knee' before teeing off in the Veterans' December Mid-Week Stableford at my club Dale Hill before it was pointed out to me by Toby 'Please Don't Make Me Putt That' Atkinson that at least half the field might struggle to get up again.

But it's about another related matter that I'm writing to you now. Have you by any chance heard of Old Tom Morris? (By the way, in no way is he connected to the main character in 'Old Tom's Cabin'). Well, Old Tom Morris is a revered figure in golf and is widely regarded as the sort of 'Grandfather' of the game credited with doing more than anyone else to establish it back in 19th century Scotland. There are loads of books about him and dozens of historic golf courses designed by him. In other words, he's a formidable target that I believe I have the ammunition to thoroughly discredit. And what a significant coup it would be for BLM if you could expose him as an evil and exploitative man.

After considerable research in his home town of St Andrews, I have uncovered scandalous revelations that will send enormous shock waves reverberating around the ordinarily genteel world of golf. In the middle of the 19th century, Old Tom Morris established his own golf equipment business manufacturing balls and clubs. And what were the latter made of do you think? Hickory wood. And where did it come from? The southern states of the USA where it was almost certainly harvested by slave labour. And so there you have it, golf's most legendary figure exposed as little better than a slave trader!

As well as tearing down all the statues of him, I think we should demand that all the courses he designed, including the

Old, New and Jubilee courses at St Andrews, be immediately closed with a view to being comprehensively redesigned in due course by a contemporary golf course architect, preferably one of colour.

○○○○○

Dear Head of the Nobel Prize Committee,

Looking through the list of Nobel prizes, I note that you dish them out for Physics, Chemistry, Physiology or Medicine, Peace, Literature and Economics. How often, if ever, have you reviewed this list since you were set-up in 1900? My suspicion is that you haven't and are consequently out of touch with current trends. Stuck in Sweden, it's perhaps hardly surprising you're unaware of what's going on in the world.

Frankly, very few of my friends or family are in the least bit interested in either Physics of Chemistry. You should do what I did at school about 65 years ago and drop them both immediately. Medicine is critical to the wellbeing of mankind and so you should definitely retain that. As a published author myself, I certainly recognise the importance of great literature but does Economics contribute anything to the sum total of human happiness? Peace is a very good thing so that should definitely stay.

Chucking out the unpopular stuff will leave you room to add some fresh subjects that are more in tune with the age. At present, you don't reward anything sporty, which is a great shame as sport is an area of human endeavour that really interests people in a way that Physics and Chemistry never can or will.

There are, of course, a lot of sports from which to choose. In your part of the world there is, for example, skiing. But winter sports are only really of interest in those places where it snows a lot. Golf, on the other hand, is played in pretty well every country on the planet. And so I urgently suggest you start a Nobel Prize for Golf. But don't give it to one of the famous players, who neither needs the money nor the recognition. Instead, give it to an unsung hero who, for example, has spent a considerable amount of time making inspired suggestions as to how the game could be improved.

One last question; is it okay to nominate oneself for a prize?

Dear Queen,

First of all may I say what a pleasure it has been to be one of your humble subjects for the past 70+ years. I honestly couldn't have asked for a nicer monarch to reign over me and my only regret is that, although I lived just the other side of Hyde Park from you for a number of years when working at the Ministry of Agriculture and Fisheries in Westminster, we never met. Sadly, unless I receive a knighthood for services to golf, and pretty sharpish because neither of us is getting any younger, it is extremely unlikely that we ever will.

However, I haven't given up all hope of seeing your regal smile close up and the Platinum Pudding competition would appear to offer what I suspect will be my very last chance. Since I hate cooking and have no significant experience of preparing puddings, I must confess it's something of a long shot – a bit like a hole in one.

And it's that almost mythical phenomenon that is the inspiration behind my recipe for 'Merriweather's Mess' which, incidentally, only uses ingredients that you might encounter either directly on a golf course or, at the very least, in a shop or off-licence close to a golf course.

The ingredients are as follows:

- Two pounds of raspberries
- Half-a-dozen free-range eggs
- One pound of self-raising flour
- Half-a-pound of castor sugar
- Four tablespoons of treacle
- Three milk chocolate bars
- Five fluid oz of gin
- Five fluid oz of kirsch
- Five fluid oz of whisky
- Five fluid oz of kummel
- Two pounds of green marzipan
- One Twiglet

Wash the raspberries and put them in a large bowl. Melt the chocolate bars on a low heat and then pour the chocolate onto the raspberries before slowly adding all the other ingredients except the marzipan. Stir with a large spoon until the mixture is reasonably firm and can be moulded into a large thick disc. Create a small round hole in the middle and then cook in a pre-heated oven at 195 degrees Celsius for half-an-hour or thereabouts. Remove from the oven and roll the marzipan flat before spreading it evenly over the top so that it resembles a green. For the final touch, shove a twiglet in the hole to represent the flagstick.

Dear Xi Jinping,

Before I explain the principal purpose of this letter, would you kindly settle an argument I'm having with my friend Dave? He thinks the 'XI' in your name means you should properly be referred to as Jinping the 11th in the same way that Louis XIV, the King of France in the middle of the 17th century, was Louis the 14th and David Love III is Davis Love the Third. But for that to be the case, I think China would have had to have been occupied by the Romans and Chinese school-children obliged to learn Latin, which I'm pretty sure never happened.

The other thing I would like to know is whether or not you have ever been mistaken for a cricket team. Although a left-arm wrist spinner's delivery that is the equivalent of the googly is sometimes called a 'chinaman', I suspect you're unfamiliar with the game. Anyhow, because there are 11 players in a cricket team and XI, as explained above, is 11, cricket teams often have XI after their name as in, for example, the Chinese National XI or the Ignore Human Rights XI.

Since I take a keen interest in what's going on in the world, I'm aware that China is seeking to expand its global influence, and why shouldn't you? Apparently, you've been doing so for quite some time mainly through offering seemingly soft loans to poorer countries to finance infrastructure projects that Chinese firms undertake. In this way, you not only make huge profits but also increase the dependence of these third world countries on you. Very clever!

Penetrating more advanced western countries has presented a greater challenge, I suspect. Okay, we know that Huawei phones are monitoring all our conversations but transcribing them and then filing them away is a ridiculously labour-intensive operation even for a country of nearly one-and-half billion people.

What I believe you should be doing is taking over key components of the social and economic fabric of these 'target' nations. Unfortunately, you've already missed out on Newcastle United which has been grabbed by the Saudis but there are other trophy assets to be had in the UK and I would urge you to despatch your Overseas Control Minister to take a look at Dale Hill Hotel and Golf Club.

For a tiny fraction of what the Saudis coughed up for Newcastle, you could secure one of the finest golf resorts in the south-east of England with two courses and no fewer than 50 bedrooms, all of which have en-suite bathrooms.

If you take my advice and buy Dale Hill, all I ask in return is that you support my bid to become club captain.

Dear Executors of the late Sir Bruce Forsyth,

As a very keen golfer, Brucie must have encountered the problem of trying to lift a ball off a bare lie with the attendant risk of sculling the ball. Not anymore. Thanks to the new club I've developed, bare lies will no longer cause concern.

With an almost razor sharp leading edge, made from cobalt-coated tungsten, this club is set to transform the scores of average handicap golfers and will enable even the humblest hacker, to have and I quote, 'a good game… good game'. Geddit?

Why, you might wonder, am I writing to you? Well, designing and manufacturing the club was comparatively easy as compared with thinking up a name for it. To be honest I needed one that suggested that the problem of a lack of natural growth – whether grass on the course or hair on the head – was one that could easily be overcome.

Brucie demonstrated that a lack of natural hair need not be an obstacle in life, but something that can easily be dealt with; in his case, with a discreet hairpiece. In the same way, a lack of grass under the ball can be overcome when you use 'The Brucie Scalper.' I like the word scalper because it not only implies surgical-like precision (scalpel) but links in almost seamlessly, if that's the word, with 'scalp', which in turn connects with hair.

The informal research I've conducted at my golf club suggests that the name is still a popular one that will help sell the product. Although 'Brucie' is not a registered trademark, and because his image will not appear on either the packaging or the advertising (unless you'd like it to), I understand that I'm not strictly required to seek your permission to use it. However, as a courtesy, I thought I should at least alert you to the existence of the product and enquire as to whether you would like to be involved in its marketing or promotion.

If nothing else, it will help sustain his memory for thousands of years to come and permanently link his name to the game he loved.

Dear Principal Trainer of Sniffer Dogs,

Am I right in assuming that a decent dog with effective nostrils can be trained to sniff out anything from drugs to dynamite, bodies to bullets and gorgonzola to golf balls? The other thing I need to know is at what age do you retire your animals – 10, 20, 30?

The reason I ask these questions is that I believe I can offer a 'second career' to one of your ageing hounds that will enable him or her to employ their olefactorial talent to good effect as well as keeping him or her active right up until the moment he or she drops down dead.

My research has confirmed a long-held suspicion of mine that there is big money to be made in finding lost golf balls. The problem has always been how to locate them when they are often buried in the deep rough. I experimented with drones but too many golfers complained they were an unwanted distraction.

Sorry he's yet to learn if a ball is lost or not.

Dogs are ideal hunters because they are comparatively easy to train, cheap to feed and no problem to look after as compared with, say, dolphins. Because of their boundless energy, they also ought to be able to keep going for at least ten hours at a time. Assuming it takes them no longer than about 30 seconds to locate and retrieve a lost ball, they could recover somewhere in the region of 1,200 balls a day. Since a quality second-hand golf ball is conservatively worth about 50p that means a decent dog could earn its handler about £600 per day or £3000 for a five-day week. Allowing for two weeks holiday a year that's £150,000 per annum less, say, £250 for dog food leaves £149,750.

Would I be correct in thinking that you would be only too happy to let one of your retiring dogs go to a caring home for free?

Dear *Golf Monthly Magazine*,

Doubtless you are aware of the growing number of publications, websites, newsletters and the like producing lists of what are termed the 'Top 100'. Because most of my life now is taken up with writing letters, I don't have the time to carry out the necessary research but my belief is that it all began with one of the golf magazines – it could even have been yours – compiling a list of the 'Top 100' golf courses in England.

Quite why, I don't know, but for some peculiar reason this generated an enormous amount of interest and courses became obsessed with either entering the 'Top 100' or, if they were already in it, on improving their ranking. And just like chefs and Michelin stars, greenkeepers at courses that dropped down or, worse still, dropped off the list frequently contemplated swallowing their own treatment for fusarium as the only honourable way of responding to the calamity.

Inevitably and inexorably other 'Top 100' lists appeared and so we had separate lists for Scotland, Ireland, Wales, Europe, etc. When the geographical spread was exhausted, list compilers switched their attention to the various different types of courses so we were then treated to the 'Top 100' links, parkland, seaside, woodland, etc.

Despite the fact that the appetite for new lists undoubtedly still exists, the supply of them has at last dried up – or has it? Having given it a reasonable amount of thought, I believe I have hit upon a rich seam of unexploited potential that offers the prospect of nothing less than doubling, (yes, doubling!) the number of lists.

It will seem pretty obvious to you when I reveal my idea – but aren't all the greatest inventions pretty obvious with the benefit of hindsight? Here we go: why doesn't your magazine pioneer the concept of the 'Bottom 100'? In practice, you will simply mimic the development of the lists that have gone before. You could start with the worst 100 courses in England and then take it from there.

Apart from anything else, I sincerely believe giving recognition to those courses that are struggling will tap into the current fashion in this country for inclusivity. Courses that were previously ignored or shunned will now be given their share of the spotlight. And can you imagine how much attention will be paid to the previously unheralded 'Worst Course in the World'?

Dear Talent Agency,

Although he had at least three pints after we were beaten 6 & 5 in the Winter Fourball Trophy, my golf partner and long-time friend Alfie Grimsdyke told me that there's good money to be made on the after-dinner, and after-lunch I presume, speaking circuit. Despite the appalling mauling in the morning, I was on good form and was busy regaling everyone with, if you'll forgive the lack of modesty, a seemingly endless succession of fascinating anecdotes and brilliant jokes when Alfie suggested I should turn pro. 'But my handicap is 19, I'll never win a European Tour event let alone a major,' I quipped. Of course, Alfie was meaning I should become a professional speaker and I seemingly misunderstood him to create the witty remark. And it's precisely that quick speed of thought and sparkling sense of humour combined with near flawless timing that I'm confident will make me enormously popular on the circuit.

Apart from speaking at the Ladies Christmas Prize-giving in 1993 and again in 2001 at the dinner following the match between the high and medium handicappers, I can't honestly claim to have a huge amount of formal experience but both speeches went down tolerably well. Obviously, I shall need to work up some material based around my 60 years (I'm 80) of playing golf that climaxed, if I may use that expression, with no fewer than two mid-week Stableford triumphs in 1983. I can also do passable impersonations of famous golfers such as Max Faulkner, Bobby Locke, Christy O'Connor Senior and Dai Rees; plus I have a fund of sparkling stories from a lifetime working in the Civil Service that I can call on if necessary.

Because I'm not very well known outside my golf club, I shall obviously need an agent to secure lucrative engagements, which is where you come in.

I'm happy to audition at your offices, or wherever is convenient for you, and am willing to talk mostly about golf for as long as you like but, I'm afraid, I can't promise to avoid repetition, deviation or hesitation (an amusing reference to 'Just a Minute' on Radio 4). If you can get me on that show it would certainly raise my profile and boost whatever fee I might command. Alfie says decent speakers receive huge fees and £5k a pop is not unreasonable and certainly a lot less pricey than, say, Tony Blair. Perhaps I could be marketed as a cheap alternative to former Prime Ministers. I'll leave that with you.

Dear Ali Khamenei, Supreme Leader of Iran,

Looking at you, I would never have guessed that you are three-and-a-half years older than Joe Biden. Of course, you don't have the stress of fighting an election every four years. In fact, since you've got the Supreme Leader's job for life, you don't have to worry about elections at all. I don't know what you think but I can't imagine your compulsory hijab policy would have won you many votes, not amongst women at least who might also regard being stoned for committing adultery a tad on the harsh side. But I don't suspect you get to be a Supreme Leader of Iran by being soft on women.

However, it's your foreign policy I'm most interested in, especially your support of Russia in its war with Ukraine. As someone who was never very popular at school and had very few friends, I can appreciate how lonely and isolated it must feel to be what they call a 'pariah' state. But supporting the horrible Mr Putin smacks of desperation and supplying him with deadly drones isn't going to endear you either to the innocent civilian population of Ukraine or the overwhelming majority of states who support plucky President Zelensky.

With unemployment high and the economy struggling, I can understand your reluctance to close your drone factories but I have an idea that'll allow you to keep them busy without killing thousands of innocent people.

Obviously you're more familiar with the Koran than the Old Testament but you may be aware of the famous quote from the Book of Isaiah, 'They shall beat their swords into ploughshares, and their spears into pruning hooks.' As a keen golfer, I would have preferred '… their swords into drivers and their spears into wedges' but sadly golf wasn't around in biblical times.

Anyway, back to your drones and my suggestion that you convert them into 'Space Caddies' that help golfers look for their balls in the rough, fly ahead to check for hazards, relay information about the wind direction and hover above opponents to distract them when they're about to hit the ball.

There are nearly 70 million golfers in the world. Okay, forget the 10 percent who are women, who should be at home cooking dinner and almost certainly wouldn't be able to operate them anyway and you still have a huge market for your 'Space Caddies'.

Finally, if you take up my idea would you kindly appoint me Supreme Leader of Iranian Drone Manufacture with a suitable salary and benefits package?

Dear Barry Hearn,

Who would have thought that an incredibly dull sport like snooker could somehow be turned into watchable television? You did it and then did the same with another equally dull activity, darts. And then, believe it or not, fishing! What a genius you must be to make televised fishing anything other than a snooze-fest. Boxing is not everyone's cup of tea but you made an absolute fortune out of blokes – and more recently women – knocking lumps out of each other. Incidentally, I'd be grateful for an opportunity at some future date to pitch a wholly original idea to you that I'm absolutely certain would prove hugely popular at the box office – Pro Celebrity Boxing! But that's for another time. Right now I want to focus on what can be done to make professional golf more entertaining.

What the game desperately needs is an injection of pace. Although slow play can be penalised, there is no real incentive to play quicker. Part of the problem stems from the fact that far too much emphasis is placed on how many shots are taken and too little on how long the round takes. Introducing an element of speed will also enable golf to shake off its unfortunate image as a sport that principally appeals to the un-athletic, elderly and overweight.

Although my main priority is to improve televised golf, some of the revolutionary changes I will shortly reveal will inevitably filter through to golf generally. Initially, however, they will be confined to a few ground-breaking events that I'm sure one of the big boys – Sky, BT Sport, Amazon Prime or Netflix – will pay fortunes to cover.

This is how I see the inaugural One Million Dollar World Speedplay Golf Championship panning out. The top ten golfing countries of the world will each be invited to enter one player. Individual countries might well choose to hold a series of national qualifying events to help select their best representative. The World Championship Final will be played over nine holes. St Andrews, with its rich history and flat terrain, would be an ideal venue.

The ten competitors – each wearing distinctive national colours and playing a matching ball – will line up across the first tee. At the sound of the starter's gun, they will tee up and tee off. No old-fashioned caddies will be allowed but each player will be permitted a trainer to administer first-aid and the like in the one-minute break between holes in much the same way as seconds do in boxing.

The object will be to finish the hole as quickly as possible. The number of shots taken is irrelevant. There will be some rules forbidding, for example, striking an opponent, but hitting his ball is permitted, as is interfering with his swing. Unlike other forms of golf, there will be very few restrictions and absolutely no etiquette.

Whoever completes the hole last will be eliminated. Thus there will be nine players on the second tee, eight on the third and so on until there will be just two to contest the final (ninth) hole.

From television's point of view, it will be very much easier and cheaper to cover since all the action – and therefore all the cameras – will be confined to one hole at a time. Another huge advantage is that, instead of dragging on for four days, it will all be over in about an hour, making it much easier to schedule. Plus there will be plenty of what conventional golf lacks… blood. With multiple golfers playing the same hole at the same time there's bound to be a great deal of jostling, the occasional serious clash and quite a lot of blood. Any TV executive worth his Armani suit will tell you that blood is good from both an audience and advertiser's point of view. By the way, helmets and body armour will be worn which opens up whole, new, exciting ranges of golf apparel. And the very physical nature of the sport will appeal to new and younger audiences as well as fresh sponsors.

With such radical proposals there will inevitably be some resistance from the stuffy old colonels in the spike bar. To them I would like to make it clear that speedplay golf is just another development of our beloved game that will happily coexist alongside strokeplay and matchplay. I'm confident that with your support it will become to golf what T20 is to cricket.

'On the tee please welcome ...' will soon be replaced with, 'On your marks, get set, tee off!'

Dear Royal Mail,

Selling stamps can't be easy these days. Although I'm prepared to make the effort to write a proper letter – which is what I'm doing right now – too many, especially the young, appear to be content with email, texts and a thing called Wotsup or something. All, it has to be said, are very much quicker than letters but they somehow lack the romance and nothing, in my opinion, beats the excitement created by that dull thud on the doormat signalling the arrival of the post.

Invariably, the anticipation immediately evaporates when you discover there's a nasty looking one from HM Revenue and

Customs, a flier from the local pizzeria and the interesting one with a handwritten envelope is not for you but those appalling people at number 24. Never mind, unless it's Saturday, there's always tomorrow.

Strictly speaking, it doesn't really matter to you if people don't write to one another as long as they keep buying stamps. In fact, you could argue that there's more profit in unused stamps than there is from those stuck on envelopes. With the former, you don't have all the hassle of having to collect, sort and deliver anything.

There are, would you believe, 60 million stamp collectors in the world. Mostly blokes and overwhelmingly socially inept individuals with serious personality disorders, they don't go out much and consequently have nothing on which to spend their money. If you leave out food and drink, nearly all their disposable income goes on buying stamps and they are absolute suckers for new issues. To exploit their almost insatiable demand, all you have to do is bring out a new issue every week.

Stamps illustrating some aspect of sport are by far and away the most popular. Since there are 53 Olympic disciplines, you could feature one of these every week of the year and be left with a perfect excuse for omitting synchronized swimming.

Golf is my area of expertise and to tee things off, as it were, I'm enclosing my suggestions for the inaugural golf issue. Rather than take the easy option of famous players and courses, I've opted for the quirky and unusual and that's why each of the four designs depicts what could be described as a disaster shot.

To acknowledge the significant contribution I'm making to your viability, you might care to consider issuing the stamps on my birthday, April 1st.

Dear Head of Sport, BBC Television,

I have an idea for a series of golf programmes, which I think you'll find extremely interesting. Provisionally titled: 'Mortimer Merriweather's World of Great Golf and Stunning Women', it follows one man's ceaseless quest to find two things:

1) the most magnificent golf course in the world, and

2) the most beautiful woman on the planet.

It works like this. Each week I will visit a different golfing destination: Hawaii, Barbados, Mauritius, California, South Africa, etc. The programme is divided into three parts. In part one, I go searching for the most beautiful woman I can find.

This will take me to beaches, nightclubs, discotheques and restaurants, basically talking to attractive women. In part two I play the most spectacular golf courses, looking for the best one. And in the final part, I play golf with the most beautiful woman on the best golf course. I'm confident it will be an enormous success because it has all the basic ingredients men look for in a TV programme.

With the help of the various tourist boards, airlines and hotels, I don't think it will cost very much to make either. Especially if we restrict ourselves to just one camera. In that regard, I have already found a very good friend, Huw, who has some experience with cameras, is very enthusiastic about the project and has agreed to film it incredibly cheaply.

Having discussed it with Huw, we reckon we'll only need one week to recce each location and then a further week for filming. I know what you're thinking: what happens if the woman I choose can't play golf? Well, I thought about that, and we can get around it by inserting an instructional element where I give the woman intensive one-on-one lessons prior to taking her out on the course.

A solid 19 handicapper, I'm well qualified to teach and the tips I'll impart will only add to the overall appeal of the programme. Much of the interest will be to see: 'how she gets on'. Judicious editing out her worst shots might be necessary.

Dear Monty

I've long been a huge fan of yours and would love to see you cap a magnificent career by capturing at least one major title. After all, Phil Mickelson, who can't be much younger than you, recently snaffled another one. What's more, I think I can help.

There's nothing I can usefully contribute on the playing front as, frankly, I struggle off a handicap of 19. But my mother taught me a valuable lesson early on in life, which I've always found useful and would like to pass on to you now. She used to say: 'Mortimer, no matter what happens, smile and be grateful you're alive.' And you know what, it truly helps.

Like most other folk I've been through a lot in my life, what with never having passed the driving test, redundancy and piles, but I've always smiled and considered myself a lucky man. Frankly, with everything you have – a great talent, pots of money and a beautiful family – you ought not to be so grumpy, especially as you probably never have to pay a green fee or rake a bunker.

Okay, you're allowed the odd scowl when you miss a short putt, but the rest of the time you should try to appreciate the glorious scenery and be happy that you're playing golf. Millions of others can't, because they're married and their wives won't let them. When was the last time Mrs M. said: 'Colin, you're not off playing golf again! You played Thursday, Friday and yesterday and now you want to play on Sunday as well.'?

To play golf as often as you do, travel all over the world, stay in the finest hotels, have all your equipment supplied free and be able to watch the best players close up, makes me very jealous. Whenever you feel fed up, just remember Agnes Merriweather and her splendid philosophy on life.

Dear Andrew 'Beef' Johnston,

Your performances on the golf course have fallen away a bit of late, as have your earnings, and so I'm hoping you might be interested in a proposal that I'm confident could make us ridiculously rich. In short, it's a revolutionary diet that could render obesity as obsolete as the mashie-niblick. Called the Golfing Diet, we will spread the word with a blockbuster of a book and reinforce the message with talks, seminars and courses.

Ironically, dieting is one of the biggest growth industries in the UK right now and golf is still benefiting from the enormous boost provided by the pandemic. Combine the two and we can't lose.

Like a lot of the other members at Dale Hill Hotel and Golf Club, I regularly put on weight every winter and just as regularly lose it the following summer. Because I only play golf once a week in the winter but three or four times in the summer, the obvious explanation is that I burn more calories playing more often. The truth, however, just like golf itself, is very much more complicated.

Teeing off in the late morning, I invariably play through lunch and am so engrossed in the game that I don't even notice the absence of food. Effectively, therefore, cutting out three of four meals a week with no effort whatsoever. Why, you might wonder, do you need a book to explain such a seemingly simple idea? The answer is that nothing is as straightforward as it at first seems and there are a number of aspects that need considerable clarification to both satisfy the reader and justify the £14.99 (hardback) price.

For example, the book will explain how you can increase from one to two rounds per day and miss even more meals. Then there is the revolutionary approach to alcohol, which is conventionally regarded, quite wrongly in my opinion, as fattening. By drinking two or three pints after a strenuous day's golf, the likelihood is that you'll fall asleep and miss even more meals.

There are other enormous advantages to the Golfing Diet. Instead of sneaking out of the house to avoid having to explain that you're off playing golf again, you can pick up your clubs, look your partner in the eye and say that you are determined to lose more weight. What kind of miserable person would withhold their support for such a worthy endeavour?

And there is the potential for vast fortunes to be made from the phenomenal spin-offs. Clinics would open up all over the country to offer those on the Golfing Diet special week-long courses. Naturally, they would need to have the basic facilities – a challenging course and a decent bar – and be approved by me as suitable establishments capable of both delivering quality service and paying an exorbitant franchise fee.

To dramatically demonstrate the efficacy of the programme, I'm afraid you will have to slim down a lot. Losing a few inches around the waist while 'Beefing' up your bank balance has to be a good move, eh? If, for whatever reason, you don't want to be involved, would you have a word with Shane Lowry for me?

Dear European Ryder Cup Committee,

After discussing it with my golf buddies and giving it considerable thought, I should like to formally declare that I wish my name to go forward as a candidate for the captaincy of the European Ryder Cup team in 2025.

Traditionally, of course, the captain has considerable experience of playing in the event. Although I've watched an awful lot of it on television and read a fair number of newspaper and magazine articles about it, I can't honestly claim to have actually played in it as such. But it is my belief that it's not really necessary to have done so. A 19-handicapper with an elegant shoulder turn but a tendency to slice, I could bring so much more to the job than some grizzled old pro whose best days are clearly behind him.

For me, the Ryder Cup would be my one and only chance of achieving true golfing glory. Although I've picked up a couple of mid-week Stablefords, I've no tour wins to fall back on. If, God forbid, Europe were to lose then I would only ever be remembered as that bumbling idiot who lost us the Ryder Cup. But I don't want to dwell on negatives, as my style of captaincy simply won't entertain the possibility of defeat.

The enormous advantage I have over all the other possible candidates is that no one, least of all the Americans, will have heard of me. They simply won't know how I'm going to play it. Strictly between ourselves, I don't yet know myself other than I probably will do quite a bit of front-loading come Sunday's singles. But I don't want to say too much as there are a lot of Yanks about and you never know who might see this.

The fact that the European players won't have heard of me either is yet another enormous plus. You see, I won't be saddled with any unhelpful baggage. To get to the top of any sport necessarily requires a single-minded determination and utter ruthlessness, neither of which are terribly attractive traits in a human being. Enemies are made, jealousy is rife and unpleasant incidents are not readily forgotten. I, on the other hand, with no relevant history whatsoever, will rise well above such squabbling and pettiness. What is more, with no preconceptions or previous experience, I am confident that I will bring a refreshing innocence to the event that I sincerely believe will blow like the proverbial breath of fresh air throughout the entire three days.

I will not, however, be quite as green as some might imagine as I skippered the Dale Hill Foxes team in the late 1980s. Open to those with a handicap between 11 and 18, we were twice runners-up in the Tunbridge Wells District League. Had Stuart 'Three Putts' Macarthy not been stricken by an appalling attack of gout on the morning of the all-important match against The Nevill, we might very well have captured the title in 1987. Furthermore, I once visited New York City on holiday and learnt a great deal about Americans and their sport; for example, how much they hate to lose and how little they understand of cricket.

Now hopefully convinced of my unique suitability for the job, doubtless you are wondering whether or not I will stay on and captain Europe again in 2027. That's a tough one to answer right now but I have to say that my instinct is to step aside and let a genuine high handicapper have a go.

Dear Greg Norman,

Luring already ridiculously rich professional golfers onto your LIV Golf Invitational Series by offering them the only thing that really matters to them viz. more money, was an undoubted masterstroke. Another attractive element in your pitch was reducing the number of rounds in each tournament from four to three because what hugely overpaid athlete would want to play 72 holes when he can earn the same obscenely fat cheque for just 54? And having no cut removes needless stress by ensuring that, however badly they play, every fat-cat competitor banks big bucks. It's a win-win for everyone.

Be honest with me: were you influenced in your decision to opt for just three rounds by your infamous final-round meltdown at the US Masters at Augusta in 1996 when you blew a six-shot lead and lost to Faldo by no fewer than five shots? And I don't suppose being responsible for the greatest Sunday crumble of all time is much consolation for missing out on what would have been your only green jacket.

And are you aware that, going into the final round, you were leading the field in no fewer than nine major championships but only converted one of those into a win (the 1986 British Open)? No wonder you prefer three rounds to four! Just 36 holes would almost certainly be even more appealing to your greedy, aging and mostly worn-out and washed-up competitors but the XXXVI Golf Invitational Series is almost impossible to pronounce and so you should perhaps stick with LIV.

You're right, too, to ignore the appalling human rights' record of your paymasters, the Saudis. Wouldn't it be hugely hypocritical of a sport that loves nothing more than a sudden death play-off to take issue with a regime for whom summary executions are simply a remarkably effective means of reducing the prison population?

Oh yes, I nearly forgot why I'm writing to you. I'm looking for part-time work that pays around £100k plus holidays and substantial benefits. Have you anything suitable?

Dear Robert Trent Jones, Jnr

My research reveals that you are 84 years old. Don't you think it's about time you dumped the 'Jnr' tag into what you Yanks call a garbage can? Anyway, you're arguably the world's leading golf course architect and a famously shrewd businessman whom I believe would love to partner me in what will undoubtedly be the most exciting development in the history of golf course design since the introduction of the flagstick in 1875, which was even before you were born!

Golfers, as you know, are desperate to lower their handicaps and will spend a fortune on equipment, lessons and anything they think might shave off a stroke or two. Although it's hard to be precise, I would guess that each shot off a handicap is worth an average of around £2,750 or thereabouts.

Without wishing to upset equipment manufacturers and teaching pros, the stark truth is that the beneficial effect of new clubs and lessons, assuming they help at all, is unlikely to be anything other than marginal and ephemeral. There is really no escaping the fact that, for most of us at any rate, golf is a ceaseless and uneven battle against seemingly overwhelming odds.

The vast majority of golfers are pretty dreadful and should by now have realised and accepted that they are never going to be any good and that their efforts to improve are inevitably doomed to failure because they simply don't have the talent. But they battle on bravely in the mistaken belief that one glorious day the sun will come out and the 'secret' will be revealed to them which, despite hitting or, rather, miss-hitting, tens of thousands of balls over the past decades, had never made itself known before.

Irrespective of how impractical and unobtainable it is, the dream of a lower handicap is an important and worthy goal to which most aspire. Unlike those pedalling the golfing equivalent of snake oil, I offer help that's both radically different from anything seen before and, most importantly, is hugely lucrative. You see, a lower handicap is just one of my ambitions; accumulating enormous wealth is another.

Before I unveil my revolutionary idea I should explain that my analysis suggests that those with handicaps between 20 and 28 should see theirs tumble to somewhere between the mid and high teens whilst those with handicaps from 13 to 19 should come down between four and six shots. Although lower handicappers would also benefit, I'm not especially concerned about them since my priority is wealthy duffers who would willingly cough up vast sums to be less self-conscious about their embarrassingly high handicaps.

My 'mission statement' is: 'It's not for golfers to make adjustments but for us to adjust to them.' So the really good news is there's no need for our customers to change their postures, realign their stances or alter their grips.

Okay, I think you are ready now for the dramatically novel 'Merriweather Golf and Country Club' concept. Although the intention is eventually to roll out several dozen all over the UK before going global, they will essentially be very similar. Broadly, each will contain four par threes of between 80 and 150 yards, 12 par fours of between 270 and 320 yards and four par fives, none of which will exceed 480 yards. Furthermore, since 85% of golfers slice the ball, the overwhelming majority of the par four and fives will dog-leg right. These same holes will not only be aligned so as to benefit from the prevailing wind but, wherever practicable, will also be downhill. Because golfers would much prefer a long uphill walk into the wind after the round than take on the elements during it, we could offer a buggy ride back to the distant clubhouse on top of the hill for a modest, say, £25.

Other interesting features of these courses will be a total absence of bunkers, water or anything remotely resembling a hazard. This will both avoid needless penalty shots as well as speed up play. And there will, of course, be no out of bounds even if this means shots having to be taken from private gardens, railway lines or busy roads. If any homeowners or authorities object, the remarkably generous local rules will permit a drop without penalty.

The fairways will be wonderfully wide with mounds on either side encouraging the ball to bounce back into the middle and, taking my cue from Augusta National, there will no rough worthy of the name. The greens will be huge and shaped like saucers. Since they won't be wasting their time raking bunkers or cutting the rough, the green staff will be able to concentrate on producing immaculate smooth greens.

Don't forget, as well as golf there will be snooker tables with enlarged pockets and tennis courts with sensibly low nets. Considering that members will be able to play on, not one, but a network of 'sympathetic' courses and will certainly slash their handicap, is £50,000 per annum too cheap?

Well, Junior, are you in?

Dear Jimmy Tarbuck,

To be honest, I've never thought you were particularly funny but my mother liked you a lot and thought you funnier than that other scouse comedian, Billy Connolly.

Anyway, whether you're funny or not is irrelevant. What matters is you're a well-known name and that you play golf because I've developed a really exciting club that I know will interest you.

Called 'The Tarby Tosser', it's a speciality club specifically designed to cope with those awkward little flop shots over bunkers and the like where getting the ball to rise quickly is the priority and not much distance is required.

The 'secret' is the 78 degrees of loft, which enables the player to strike the ball really hard without fear of flying it through the green. The only serious problem we've encountered in the research and development stage is that sometimes the ball flies almost vertically off the face of the club and has on occasions struck the player both on the way up and, less frequently, on the way down.

To overcome this and obviate the risk of someone getting badly hurt and suing us, we've had to incorporate a shield. Originally this was made of the same steel/titanium alloy as the clubface but we soon discovered that, being opaque, it prevented the player from seeing the ball both at address and impact. We therefore switched to Perspex, which works fine except that occasionally the ball strikes the screen, which is good insofar as it protects the player but bad in that the ball bounces straight back down either onto the ground or, worse still from a scoring point of view, back onto the clubface, which technically constitutes a double hit and incurs a penalty stroke.

My real purpose in writing to you is to enquire as to whether you would wish to become involved in this project as an investor and/or promoter.

Dear Deposed President Donald Trump,

Having had a bike nicked from outside my flat in West Hampstead 20 years ago, I can understand how you must feel about having an election stolen from you. The worst thing about it all is that it undermines your faith in humanity and you probably don't feel you can trust people anymore. It must be especially hard for you coming as it does after so many of your aides, assistants and advisors, not to mention that dodgy lawyer of yours who was sent to prison, all jumped ship. You gave them respectable jobs in the White House and a chance to move on from their previous involvement in fraud, tax evasion, money-laundering and general criminality and they thank you by dumping you in it. No wonder you got on so well with that nice Mr Putin, who also has good reason to be somewhat paranoiac.

Anyway, my advice is to abandon any idea of running again, forget the whole presidential thing and move on to something for which you have a real passion: golf. I think you'll find that, relieved of the responsibility of leading the western world, your short game will benefit and the time saved by not having to attend boring cabinet meetings and tedious summit conferences will allow you to work on your swing. In the fullness of time you might well look back at the humiliation of not being granted a second term as a blessing.

Because you're in the hotel and hospitality industry, you will also be able to claim any green fees, trolley hire and range balls against tax. Oops, I was forgetting you don't pay tax. Never mind, not claiming any tax relief on these items can only enhance your image and silence those miserable critics within the golf industry – almost certainly high handicappers – who claim you're a megalomaniac just because you acquired Turnberry, Doonbeg and Doral and re-christened them Trump Turnberry, Trump Doonbeg and Trump National Doral.

Finally, there is an under-exploited course on the east coast of Scotland that is simply crying out for a massive overhaul and makeover. Not only that but it also regularly hosts the British Open and is so embedded in the rota that even those snotty suits at the R&A won't be able to deny you the thrill of hosting the greatest golf tournament in the world. How does, 'The Open at St Trumps' sound to you?

Dear Mystery Shopping Company,

As I understand it, you employ people to walk furtively into shops and discreetly buy a range of goods without at any time revealing their identity. These 'spies' then secretly report back to you and, in return, are allowed to hang on to all the stuff they've purchased. You let the shop know how well or badly they're doing as regards 'customer experience' as well as identifying any especially surly shop assistants who are then unceremoniously sacked immediately. Have I got that about right?

Well, I would like to suggest that you expand your field of operation beyond the retail sector to a totally different area of human endeavour where customers are often treated with unacceptable contempt and disdain – golf clubs.

There are a number of indicators that all golfers are familiar with that let the visitor know whether

a) they are genuinely welcome;
b) the club are somewhat ambivalent in that they want their money to help keep the members' subscription down but would prefer it if they just paid the green fee and didn't actually venture onto the course; *or*

c) they will be met with unbridled hostility because the filthy rich and stuck-up members seriously hate visitors.

SIGNAGE

a) Clear signs to the club from at least one mile away.
b) A modest sign 200 yards away pointing in the direction of the club.
c) A very discreet almost unnoticeable sign at the entrance

CAR PARK

a) Everyone uses the same car park.
b) There's a members' car park and an adjacent visitors' car park.
c) The visitors' car park is at least half-a-mile from the clubhouse.

CHANGING ROOMS

a) There's one large, comfortable changing room for everyone.
b) There's a medium-sized changing room for members and a marginally smaller one for visitors.
c) There is an enormous, carpeted, oak-panelled changing room with spacious lockers and numerous showers for members and a tiny, cramped, smelly changing room with a splinter-ridden wooden floor, two metal hangers and one (out of order) shower for visitors.

BARS

a) There is one well-appointed, carpeted bar with two cheery barmaids and bowls of peanuts routinely offered to all drinkers.
b) There is a comfortable members' bar and a rather less comfortable visitors' bar.

c) Visitors are only permitted to purchase drinks through the serving hatch on the balcony provided they can catch the attention of the wholly disinterested barman.

PRACTICE FACILITIES

a) Everyone is welcome to use the practice facilities.
b) Members may hit off the grass on the range while visitors must use the mats.
c) The covered bays on the range are for the exclusive use of members as is the short-game area. The immaculate putting green close to the first tee is for members only while visitors may use the poorly-mown patch behind the car park that, since it only has one hole cut into it, cannot accommodate more than one golfer at a time.

TEE TIMES

a) Visitors are welcome at all times.
b) Visitors are welcome on weekdays but not at weekends.
c) Visitors are only tolerated on weekday afternoons after 3pm except Tuesdays (Ladies Day) and Thursdays (Seniors Day) when, if they enter the premises, they risk being shot.

Providing you pay my green fees and all expenses, I am willing to act as your full-time mystery golfer.

Dear Editor of the *Times*,

Although I read the *Telegraph*, I think it would be altogether more fitting if, when the time comes, my obituary were to appear in your paper which, albeit a bit left-wing for my taste, is a respected journal of record. My birth appeared in the

Times in 1936 as did my ill-fated marriage in 1960 and so it would be appropriate if, following my demise, you carried an authoritative account of my life.

To make it easier for you, I have drafted my own obituary, which I affirm is both fair and accurate.

Born in Bagshot in 1936, Mortimer Winstanley Fortescue Bertram Merriweather was the only child of Colonel Archibald Merriweather of the King's Royal Hussars and Agnes Mablethorpe. Following somewhat reluctantly in his father's illustrious footsteps, Merriweather attended Eton College before going on to East Basildon Polytechnic where he gained a Diploma in Woodwork and was voted 'Toff of the Year' by his fellow students in 1957.

The following year he joined the Civil Service as a clerical officer at the Ministry of Agriculture, Fisheries and Food, a post he held for 43 years without ever being seriously considered for promotion. Although enormously frustrated at work, his loyalty to the Crown was so strong that he never considered leaving.

Away from his cramped office, Merriweather devoted most of his time to the game of golf without ever achieving much in the way of progress. His handicap stubbornly hovered in the low to mid 20s. Nevertheless, his fertile imagination resulted in a number of original ideas to improve the game. Much to his regret, none of these ever came to anything.

Another huge disappointment was his failure to be elected captain of his beloved golf club, Dale Hill. Despite campaigning tirelessly throughout his more than half-century at the club, the closest he came in the ballot was third out of four when the person he just edged into last place was exposed as a convicted paedophile.

This Is The Last Will And Testament Of Mortimer Winstanley Fortescue Bertram Merriweather

Being of sound mind and body I hereby bequeath the following:

- £1000 to Dale Hill Hotel and Golf Club to fill in that intensely annoying little bunker just in front of the 13th green.

- £500 to Dale Hill Hotel and Golf Club to pay for a bench to be situated behind the 5th tee and a further £100 to pay for a plaque with the following inscription: *'On July 18th, 1991 Mortimer Merriweather came the closest he ever managed to a hole-in-one when striking a five iron from this tee with the ball finishing a mere three inches (7.62cms) from the hole.'*

- My TaylorMade set of clubs together with the attached umbrella, pitch-mark repairer, towel and folding trolley to the Golf Museum at St Andrews.

- All my golf balls, including the three unopened sleeves of Top-Flites, to the driving range at Dale Hill Hotel and Golf Club.

- All my golf clothes including several pairs of plus fours, numerous Argyll sweaters and far too many flat caps, to be returned from whence they came, the Help the Aged charity shop in Tunbridge Wells High Street.

- All my golf magazines dating back to 1954 with their useless advice on how to cure a slice, to the wastepaper skip at Mountfield Recycling Centre in East Sussex.

- The 100+ equally useless instruction videos and CDs into the household waste skip at Mountfield Recycling Centre.

- All my golf books including, *How to Break 100 without Breaking Sweat*; *Cure the Shanks*; *Don't Ever Yip Again*; *Say Goodbye to Three-Putting* and *The Secrets of Club Captaincy* to Tunbridge Wells Lending Library.

- After I've expired, my body will be cremated and the ashes to be delivered to Dale Hill Hotel and Golf Club by Hermes and my ashes split into three roughly equal portions and disposed of as follows:

  One lot to be deposited in the big bunker guarding the sixth green. I always struggled to escape from it. Having been responsible for removing so much of the sand it would be nice to give something back, as it were.

  Another lot should be unceremoniously dumped in the lake to the left of the ninth fairway to join the vast number of balls I deposited there over the course of more than half a century.

  The final lot should be scattered on the green of the par five 11th, upon which I so nearly sank the only putt for eagle that I ever had in my entire life. In asking this I recognise that, from the perspective of the rules of golf, I may for evermore be deemed a loose impediment and dealt with accordingly.

Dear Merlin Unwin Books,

As a reward for passing 'O'-level English, my parents gave me a signed copy of James Joyce's *Ulysses*. Unfortunately, it was signed by them and not Mr Joyce. Never mind. This was in 1952 and I'm still only on chapter four. The point I'm making is that I'm not a voracious reader which, since you publish books, is probably not the sort of thing you want to hear.

Slightly more encouraging from your point of view is that, if I were to read more books, I would most probably read yours as you seem to specialise in stuff about the countryside, natural history and what I would call 'fresh air pursuits' like hunting, shooting and fishing. Well, hunting has been banned which, since I gather your offices are in Ludlow, is news that may not have reached you yet. Apologies for dropping that bombshell but I can offer what I trust is an acceptable alternative to chasing vermin and that is the Royal and Ancient game of golf.

Before you point out that you don't have any gifted golf writers among your authors, permit me to offer my services. Although in 1968 I had a letter published in *Golf Illustrated* highlighting the difficulty procuring made-to-measure plus fours, it would be a slight exaggeration to describe me as a published author. However, and here's the really good news, I have written what I honestly believe is certain to be a colossal best-seller.

Two Ruddy Ducks and a Partridge on a Par Three is a sparkling collection of fascinating letters written to various heads of state, showbiz celebrities, religious leaders, golf professionals, companies and organisations. They contain utterly original ideas and brilliantly imaginative suggestions to improve the game of golf.

There are nearly one million golfers in the UK: if only half of them buy the book I calculate that I would earn sufficient to pay my annual subscription to Dale Hill with enough left over for a three-bedroom detached house on the outskirts of Tunbridge Wells. I don't know what property prices are like in Ludlow but there's surely every chance you could afford to expand your offices and open a dedicated golf section with, subject to acceptable terms and conditions, me at the head of it.

Ed: usual rejection letter please.

'Clive Agran is golf's funniest writer'.
John Hopkins, former *Times* golf correspondent

Clive Agran is known for his regular contributions
to all the top golf magazines in the UK including
Today's Golfer, National Club Golfer, Golf Monthly and
Golf News. For several years he had a regular opinion
column in *Golf Monthly* before switching
his allegiance to *Golf International*.

His style is light-hearted and whimsical and his
columns are always amusing.

His popularity spread overseas through his regular
features in *Sports Illustrated* and *Kingdom* in the
USA, *Golf Digest Middle East* and *Swing* (Singapore).
He has also written for *travelgolf.com worldgolf.com
Golfshake* and *The World's Greatest Golf Destinations*.